HERE FOR THE RIDE

*Ten Invitations from Jesus to the
One Who Longs for More*

Carrie Ellen

Here for the Ride: Ten Invitations from Jesus to the One Who Longs for More

Shining Roots Publishing
© 2026 by Carrie Ellen
Print Edition

All rights reserved. No part of this book may be reproduced or used in any manner without the prior written permission of the copyright owner, except for the use of brief quotations in a book review.

All Scripture quotations, unless otherwise indicated, are taken from the Holy Bible, New International Version®, NIV®. Copyright ©1973, 1978, 1984, 2011 by Biblica, Inc.™ Used by permission of Zondervan. All rights reserved worldwide. www.zondervan.com The "NIV" and "New International Version" are trademarks registered in the United States Patent and Trademark Office by Biblica, Inc.™

Book Cover Design by ebooklaunch.com
Typeset by: Paul Salvette
Copyediting by: Jessica Snell (jessicasnell.com/editing)

Library of Congress Control Number: 2025927619

ISBN: 979-8-218-89620-1 (print)
ISBN: 979-8-218-89621-8 (ebook)

To the Pilot:

What an adventure we've been on! I'm so thankful for our life and family that we've built together. No one makes me laugh like you. May we, and the future generations of our family, say yes to the invitations of Jesus.

Table of Contents

Foreword	ix
Introduction: *Here for the Ride*	1
1. The Invitation	11
2. Invited to Slow Down	25
3. Invited to Lose Control	39
4. Invited to Live the Better Way	53
5. Invited to Walk and Talk with Jesus	65
6. Invited to Cast Your Cares	79
7. Invited to Today	93
8. Invited to Give It Up	109
9. Invited to Peace	119
10. Invited to Run Home	131
11. Invited to Flourish	141
Conclusion	153
Acknowledgments	161
Notes	165
More from Carrie	169
About the Author	171

Foreword

There are many good books out there that instruct you on the basic principles of the Christian life. You can learn something from most of them, but the vast majority are little more than instruction manuals, offering a lot of "how-to" advice but lacking in personal connection.

That's why *Here for the Ride* is so refreshing. While Carrie Ellen's newest book contains plenty of practical advice on how to live out your life as a follower of Jesus, she also brings herself into the narrative—not enough to make it all about Carrie, but more than enough to paint a picture of a healthy, relatable lifestyle of discovering and rediscovering the way of Jesus.

The premise of *Here for the Ride* is that "Jesus has given us everything we need to get through every situation and every circumstance we face every day because he's given us his Spirit to serve as our guide every step of the way."

Carrie brings this premise to life by sharing a series of personal encounters, such as:

- Trekking along a trail in Red Rock State Park with her husband and two boys, whom she affectionately calls the "J Men." On this trail she comes to realize what it means to embark on a new path and trust Jesus to lead her gently but firmly along.
- Having a fervent desire to serve Jesus in Africa which Jesus did not fulfill—instead, he brought her an African husband.
- Experiencing the tyranny of being overly busy and being prompted by the Spirit to slow down enough to hear God's voice.

Blended into these stories is an abundance of sound teaching—not surprising when you consider Carrie's seminary training. I was impressed and inspired by a recurring biblical theme that is mostly overlooked in the church today: *surrender*. Church leaders love to talk about the victorious Christian life and the truth that we are "more than conquerors through him who loved us." Yes, those are critically important doctrinal realities. But before we can conquer and be victorious, we must surrender to him who loved us. Carrie's perspective on what it means to surrender to Jesus is timely and refreshing.

Ultimately, the "ride" Carrie takes us on is a wonderful metaphor for the journey of a maturing follower of Jesus. Or as she describes it, "a joyful sprint toward what matters most." Now that's what I call a *ride*!

—Stan Jantz

INTRODUCTION

Here for the Ride

In my first book, *That's For Sure*,[1] I told the story of when my two sons and I took a two-mile night hike through a beautiful nature center in McKinney, Texas. It was dark. We didn't know our surroundings very well, but we had a guide, and he led us and about fifteen other hikers.

We started out on a dirt path through a grove of trees, crossed wooden and iron bridges with lakes below, and went through marshland filled with six-foot-tall reeds of grass. We saw deer grazing in an open field and heard birds singing their evening song. It was beautiful and it was dark. Without our guide and his subtle red light, we would have been terribly lost.

His light was all the invitation we needed in

order to follow.

And in its simplest form, that's what this book is about. Jesus is all the light we need. Gazing upon him will help us to see things rightly. His light and lead invite us to follow and to find our footing upon him and his ways.

The words on the pages that follow are for those of us who know Jesus is good, who believe him at his word, and who desire to live according to his plan and purpose, yet who simultaneously long for more.

The chapters to come are for those who often feel lost and alone in the dark—for the ones who believe it's up to us to figure everything out in life, forge our own way, and make the best of what comes at us and our families.

Culturally, we are made to feel we have to navigate our own way, and because of this false narrative unjustly placed upon our shoulders, we are often inclined to spend a significant amount of time searching for what we think or feel we need to remain safe, secure, and satisfied in a cutthroat world.

But that narrative is just not true at all. We do not have to stumble and feel our way through the dark. We are not left on our own to live our truth and follow our hearts. That's an icky baloney sandwich without an ounce of health in it. We live in a culture that screams lies in our faces about who we are, who we can be, and who we ought to be. We're led to believe every decision in life is up to us to make. That's a lot of pressure, and it doesn't take more than a glance around to see that much of the culture we find ourselves in today is feeling that pressure and is completely overwhelmed by it.

However, when we quiet the shouts of lies from a world that can never satisfy us or make us whole and healthy, our ears are free to hear Jesus and our eyes are better able to focus on him.

Jesus has given us everything we need to get through every situation and every circumstance we face every day because he's given us his Spirit to serve as our guide every step of the way.

He's given us his word, which is full of wisdom about life's circumstances and insight into who he is and what he cares most about.

He's given us community found in the family of God—in church settings, in nonprofit organizations, and in those doing his work throughout the world.

We may have been born into a dark and chaotic world, but Jesus, because of his deep care and compassion for all people, left the glory of heaven so that his light might shine brightly in our dark world.

Jesus was born into humanity as a light in a dark place. The light of Christ literally pierced the night sky as he entered the human story, and his arrival declared good news and hope to the world through newborn baby cries.

Jesus said, "I am the way and the truth and the life."[2] He is the compass we absolutely need to know which way to go, where to go, and how fast or slow to move in life.

Living in him and with him by our side is a much better way to live than succumbing to the pressures to navigate this life according to what we think is best.

This book is an encouragement to keep listening and looking for Christ in life. It's a reminder to bend our ears towards what he says is true and to train our eyes to see as he sees. It's about saying yes to the invitations he constantly extends to live the better way—*his* way, a way that goes beyond feelings and circumstance.

We have all the necessary tools in place to live in the fullness that he created us for and that he purposed for us long before he laid the foundations of the earth.

This book is a reminder and an encouragement to draw what we need from the tools that we already have in front of us, to free us from our desire to control and be in charge of our lives and the people closest to us.

This book is a call to freedom. Freedom found only in Jesus and his way. It's a call to walk through life openhandedly, expectantly, and to take courage and move forward, despite fears, setbacks, and failures.

This little book is a reminder that we are no longer our own. We've been bought with a price and are too valuable to waste our lives looking anywhere other than to the one who rescued us, redeemed us, and is forever renewing us into who he created us to be. We are Christ's ambassadors. We live for him—not for ourselves or for anyone else, but for Christ and Christ alone.

What if surrendering our life's expectations and our desires to Jesus opens us up to embrace him and find all of who we are and all we need in him?

Jesus has given us all so that we might know him, walk in his ways, experience joy, peace, adventure, and freedom, and step into the person he made us to be.

Ultimately, *Here for the Ride* is about discovering or rediscovering the way of Jesus. His way is better than any way we could possibly try to forge on our own and apart from him. Together, we'll uncover how his way is better through looking at the many invitations Jesus extends to every one of us to follow him, to trust him, and to believe him in all things and for our good.

He longs to lead us, and he designed us to start each day with a *Here for the Ride* mentality. We need to recognize him in all areas of our lives, walking with us through all circumstances and situations we find ourselves in, and we need to trust him regardless of the outcome.

Jesus designed our ears to hear his gentle whisper over the shouting of our inner monologues. With Jesus, we no longer have to rely on ourselves to say what we think we need to hear to survive our days. Jesus can and wants to lighten our load, to be the one and only one we rely upon.

And the best part is, he's incredibly patient. He does not rush us or get upset when we take a hot minute to understand and to go where he leads. And, even better news, when we stray off course—because we all have our moments—his mercy and kindness continually course correct us as he constantly invites us back to his side.

And yet, even better news than that, when we're flat-out defiant towards him (oh, just me?) and adamant that we've *got this* one without him, his grace is enough to bring us back the moment we realize we actually don't have this at all.

It's true that the path walked with Jesus is a path that leads to freedom, joy, and contentment. But the even more overwhelming truth is that we do not need to wait until we reach the destination of heaven to receive the prize at the end of the race. It's *on the path* walked with Christ right now that we experience joy, peace, and fullness despite circumstance.

We don't have to wait for kingdom come to experience the sweetness of surrender. We get to experience freedom and joy and peace right here, right now, with every step walked in step with the Spirit of God.

Dear reader and friend, I am so glad this book made its way into your hands. It's often true that authors write books that they themselves need the most. I need this book and I hope you do too. I need the reminder that Jesus' way is so much better than my own, not only for me, but for all the people around me. Especially the ones I'm in charge of feeding and keeping alive and out of the ER every day. Boy mom here, so ER visits are a fear of mine on a daily basis.

The world is full of empty promises that leave us unfulfilled, unsatisfied, and oftentimes confused. Jesus is the creator of true promises designed to keep us close. Only he can satisfy us, give our weary and tired souls the rest we crave, and keep us on a path of peace.

Jesus has a better way for us to live because he *is* the better way. Even now, his invitation to follow him and find all we need in him stands. I want to live a life that reflects that I'm *Here for the Ride*: I don't have it all together, but I know and trust the one who does and who I am glad is in the driver's seat.

On the pages that follow, you'll read stories from my own life that I hope resonate with you. My hope is that you can relate to them. I know I'm not the only one who has wrestled with what it truly looks like to live a life surrendered to Christ in a world that closes in on us, pressuring us to do and live only as we see fit.

I long to taste the sweetness of surrender and I'm guessing you do too.

I hope you see yourself in my stories and are left encouraged and inspired to throw your hands up in surrender and say yes to the invitations and adventure Jesus has designed for you, not just once in your life, but in every single livelong day. Together, I think we'll discover that true freedom and flourishing in life is found on the path where Jesus walks. As we tune our ears to recognize his voice above all other voices, we'll begin to have clearer sight of the plans and purposes he's designed uniquely for us.

The chapters that follow are stories from my real, oftentimes boring, mundane, and very ordinary, life. I'm writing from a posture of trying to figure out what it means to surrender—to grab hold of the abundant life Jesus talks about and live in peace, and I'm doing it right beside you.

I have zero advice to offer, but I have oodles of encouragement to fling your way. We're in this together, friend.

My hope for you, dear reader, is that as you make your way through this book, page by page and word by word, you fall deeply in love with Jesus and are moved by his affections for you in a way that fills you up and leaves you overflowing with joy, freedom, and peace. You've been made on purpose for a purpose uniquely designed for you by Jesus. My desire and hope for you as you read the pages that follow are that you are left with a renewed longing for Jesus and the red letters of your Bible.

His words are life. His invitations are for all of us. Together, may we live into the fullness of all he has to offer.

I'm here for the ride. Are you with me?

CHAPTER 1

The Invitation

The first time I heard Jesus inviting me into something new came when I least expected it and in a place I would never have guessed.

My family and I were in Arizona, ready and eager to explore the red rocks of Sedona. Hands down, Red Rock State Park is one of the most fun and adventurous hikes we've taken as a family.

Our two sons, whom I'll refer to as the J Men throughout this book, were pretty young at the time of our adventure in Arizona. Our oldest was less than a week away from turning seven and our youngest was a just a month out from turning two. I knew he wouldn't remember the trip any more than he remembered the day he arrived on this earth, giving our family more joy than we imagined possible, but I planned to take a million photos (as moms do) so he would have plenty of evidence that he was indeed there.

Needless to say, I was excited for this little family vacation together. And we had a blast. All was very normal and expected with the trip. The Grand Canyon was vast and breathtaking. It was really cold and foggy on the morning of our visit, but as soon as that fog lifted up, the views were incredible.

Sedona was indeed full of red rock, and the beauty of the place was overwhelming in the best possible way.

And while so much of the trip was very normal and went as planned, something very unexpected happened too. On the morning of December 28, 2020, we hiked a beautiful trail in Red Rock State Park, and little though I knew it at the time, Jesus was about to invite me to hang out with him in a way I'd never experienced before.

Sometimes Jesus rips into our lives in unexpected ways. Have you ever experienced him when you weren't looking for him? I love that he shows up for us always, even when we forget he's with us.

The trail led us along paths of red dirt, up to

high points with stunning views of Cathedral Rock and low into valleys surrounded by Goliath rocks and desert trees. It was breathtakingly beautiful. We were surrounded by Sedona's beauty on all sides.

We were about halfway through our hike when something completely unexpected happened: I began to sense a strong urge to read 1 Peter in my Bible.

This sort of thing didn't happen to me. It never had before and it hasn't since. I don't typically move about my days with a strongly felt need to read a specific book, chapter, or verse of the Bible.

Because this was a new feeling and experience for me, my natural instinct was to brush it off. Maybe I should have had another cup of coffee before we left the hotel that morning. Maybe I was hungry and just needed a sandwich.

For most of the hike, I tried to suppress the urge to read 1 Peter. If I just ignored it, it would go away and I could go back to hiking with my family and thinking only about the beauty that surrounded us, right? Wrong. That's not at all how the day unfolded.

Instead of pushing the thoughts and need to read 1 Peter aside, I felt surrounded not only by red rock, but by the God who literally spoke the red rock into existence. And I knew I would not be able to rest until I cracked my Bible open to 1 Peter.

My longing for my Bible grew with every step forward on the red dirt path. Jesus was extending an invite my way, and I had to decide if I was going to say yes or brush it off as fatigue or indigestion.

We were two hours from our hotel and from where my Bible was sitting in my suitcase. You may be wondering why I didn't just pull my phone out of my pocket and look it up online right then and there. And, sure, I could have done that, but that didn't feel right. I needed to have my Bible in my hands. And I needed the time to question God and work out this sense of urgency I felt for the words of Peter's first letter.

Is this for real, God? Are you really wanting me to read 1 Peter? That seems very specific. Are you sure? Is this just all in my head?

On any given day, I typically pick a specific time and place to read my Bible. I read it in my own way and on my own time. The overwhelming feeling of needing to read a specific book on a specific day felt very foreign to me—let alone the idea of taking that feeling seriously and doing it.

Most days, I'm on autopilot. How about you? I have my routine and I pretty much stick with it day in and day out. I'm up to good things in the world and have to admit, because my life is made up of mostly good activities and commitments, within the church and outside the church, that I can easily coast through life without awareness of Jesus, or worse, without consulting with Jesus at all.

I know I'm not alone in this because I hear all the time from fellow Christians how distant God feels or how quiet he seems, especially in times when they're going through something difficult and painful.

Why is this? Why do we try our very best to make wise choices, to do the right thing, to show up for our families, be a good friend and a careful neighbor, make time for Bible study, serve when needed at our church and still feel distant from God?

I don't have all the answers, friend, but I've been there. A lot. We work hard to be good people who do good things, and yet, does God see us? Does he care? Does he know us by name and does he know the desires of our hearts?

The short answer is yes.

The year before the Arizona trip, I had been asking and pleading—okay, so it was more like begging—for God to show me he loved me. Not in a God-loves-the-whole-world-so-of-course-that-includes-me kind of way, but in a deeply personal way, a way that showed me beyond a shadow of doubt that he loved bushy-browed, wild-haired, and wild-at-heart Carrie Ellen—me as I actually, really am.

It's been five years since that day in Red Rock State Park, and I am confident that the nudging I felt to read the Word of God that day was an act of kindness from God. He had heard the longing in my heart to be confident of his presence and care in my life, and he showed up before me on a path of red dirt. He called me by name and revealed his deep care for my life.

And he calls your name and cares deeply for you and your life's circumstances in this moment, right this second and in the next minute too.

That thing on your heart, weighing you down and keeping you up night? Have you talked to Jesus about it? Like really talked, with honesty and sincerity, about how you feel?

Sometimes we're so busy doing all the right

things that we can miss the very best thing there is: an open line of communication with the God who formed us, knows us intimately, and loves us beyond comprehension.

Back in Sedona, despite my attempts to shush and hush the sense of urgency, I couldn't shake the overwhelming nudge to pick up my Bible and read.

It's been a minute since that day in Sedona and while I didn't understand what was happening at the time, I have come to see and learn that God was inviting me to listen to his voice and to respond in obedience in a new way.

There's beauty to behold in yielding to the leading of the Spirit of God.

As I walked the trails of Red Rock State Park, overwhelmed by God's creation in that place and full of gratitude for experiencing it with my family, God graciously extended an invitation for me to meet with him.

I could have easily brushed off the voice I heard, assuming it was indigestion or middle-aged-lady hormones and chose not to read 1 Peter that day. That would have been so simple for me to do and would be my natural bent on any given day.

But I am so glad I didn't brush it aside and discount the urgency I felt pressed upon me to sit down, take a deep breath, crack open my Bible, flip the pages to 1 Peter, and read. I've never read Scripture with such expectancy for what the Lord might have for me as I did that day in a little hotel room in Prescott, Arizona.

This out-of-the-ordinary invitation, extended my way by the Spirit of God on that late December day in 2020, was the beginning of a new trailhead. It was the forging of a new path, one I would walk full of eager anticipation and expectation for what God might have for me and my family.

It was also the catalyst that caused me to begin to view the idea of yielding to God and surrendering to his way before mine as something sweet to participate in, instead of feeling reluctant and annoyed by the interruption, which had been my typical MO.

While I have no doubt Jesus never ceases to invite us into deeper faith and stickier trust in him always, this moment in Arizona was, for me, the kindling of a desire deep within my gut to hear the sweet voice of Jesus and to surrender to him, even if what I heard was inconvenient and didn't make sense.

Especially if what I heard didn't make sense.

I understand now and believe it was in this

moment, surrounded by red rocks, that Jesus, in his kindness, began to allow me to taste the sweetness of surrender. And he did so through an invite to meet with him in 1 Peter. But invitations from Jesus are never just about the invite. They demand a response. He extends an invite to us to a better way and it's up to us to respond. Will we say yes to what Jesus says is the better way to live or will we continue to forge our own way? Will we slow down to hear him or will we continue to switch on autopilot so we can make it through one more hectic day?

Saying yes to his invitations to live a better way will only ever lead us to more of him. And Jesus is about the business of being near his people, of standing before them, calling out the names of the ones he loves, and of leading them in accordance with his plan and purpose in the world. I believe he deeply desires to be known by his people and for his people to be overwhelmed by his love in unique ways that reveal how deeply relational he is.

He doesn't want us walking through life without him. He longs to be near his people. This truth about his loving nature is evident throughout the biblical narrative, from the days he walked beside Adam and Eve in the Garden of Eden until his glorious return and the day he draws us near to him for all eternity.

His affection is for you, dear reader. And he will stop at nothing to draw you close and invite you to walk with him throughout your life, on top of the peaks and deep down in the pits, and through all the mundane moments in the middle, with your eyes fixed on him before and beside you.

Adele Ahlberg Calhoun puts it this way: "God is a being who invites interaction."[1]

He longs for interactions with you and me. He invites us all to himself no matter where we are. For some, you may hear his invite in a busy coffee shop. Others may hear him in the laundry room on a stormy day. For me, he chose to speak while I was in Sedona.

After a full day of hiking and basking in the glory that is Sedona, AZ, my family and I made it back to our hotel. I got everyone fed and happy, and then I sat down in the stiff hotel chair, turned the old lamp beside me on, and opened my Bible to 1 Peter. I had no idea what to expect as I read. I only knew I was eager to hear from the Lord and ready to listen.

I read through the first twelve verses and looked for clues as to what I might be looking for in Peter's words to the first generation of Christ followers. Peter's words are full of confidence in Jesus, our living hope. I was encouraged by his words, yet something changed when I got to verse thirteen. The words seem to light up on the page of my Bible, as if my mind used a highlighter on verse thirteen: "Therefore, with minds that are alert and fully sober, set your hope on the grace to be brought to you when Jesus Christ is revealed at his coming."[2]

Why did this verse jump off the page for me that December day in the Grand Cayon state? I wish I knew.

I still don't fully understand all the Lord had for me that day and why this specific verse seemed to jump off the page before me, but looking back and knowing the journey he has set my family upon since, I believe it was in this moment that my eyes were opened to see and my ears opened to hear the sweet invitation Jesus extended to me to receive more of him.

This experience only caused me to start craving to hear more from Jesus, like I did that day in Sedona.

The irony for me that day was the fact that I was literally walking a beautiful path, surrounded by the glory of Jesus and his creative hand, yet, despite the beauty around me and as I walked the path before me, in life in general, I had been walking according to my way and what I thought was best for me and my family. Could I have spent more time considering and consulting with Jesus not just for the big stuff in life, but in the small too? Absolutely yes, I could have.

It's so easy to go through life on autopilot, mostly because it seems like we have no other choice but to be responsible and get stuff done. Often without realizing it, we tend to set the controls on auto and move about our days without much thought of anything, except what to make for dinner again, and then it starts all over again the next day. We're left defeated and depleted and knowing there has to be a better way.

And there is. Cue the marching band, confetti, and jazz hands. There is a better way to live, and it has everything to do with tuning our ears to hear Jesus and his word and focusing our eyes on his presence.

That day in Sedona, Jesus was clearly inviting me to walk the path of obedience and to heed his voice.

His invitation was about a return to him—a

homecoming, really. And his invitation was to hear him and do what he says. My experience is unique to me, but his invite to spend time with him is extended to everyone.

Jesus invites all of us to yield to his voice, to follow as he leads, and to do as he says because his ways are just better than ours. He knows what's best for us and desires to free us from the weight of this world and to draw us near to him, so that he can show us he's all we need to live a full and flourishing life.

Sitting in the hotel chair with my Bible open to the pages of 1 Peter, I felt as if my arms were up in the air in surrender. They weren't literally up in the air. That would have freaked my husband and kids out. But the arms of my heart were stretched out, palms up, in a posture of surrender.

I thought, *Okay, Lord. I think you're inviting me to join you in 1 Peter. I'm here and I'm listening. What's next?*

He didn't give me an audible reply. That would've really freaked my husband, my kids, *and* me out. Instead, I felt peace in my heart and like I could finally rest after a day of feeling pressed to read the Scriptures. And I realized how much I wanted to hear from God so clearly more often.

Do you feel the same? Are you longing to hear from him but struggling to do so on a daily basis? You're not alone. I'm there too. Keep reading. We can tune our ears to hear and our eyes to see despite our circumstances.

Jesus invites us to live a better way.

CHAPTER 2

Invited to Slow Down

Have you ever gotten in your car and arrived at a destination, only to have no idea how you got there? You couldn't remember the lights you sat at or the turns you made, but you managed to get to your destination? Your mind was somewhere else and autopilot kicked in. We've all been there. Our lives are so busy and full that most days all we can do is simply get through it before collapsing on the bed at night, only to get up the next day and go right back into autopilot.

If you got up this morning and remembered to put pants on, I applaud you. The struggle is real.

Not only are our lives busy and our days full, we are also bombarded with news, marketing ads, and social media posts. I'm one of those who can't stand to see notifications pop up on my phone every three seconds, so I have them turned off. Whatever it is can wait until I'm ready to take a look on my own time. Otherwise, I'd be more overwhelmed than I already am on any given Tuesday.

Busyness and distractions are a struggle for a lot of us. It's hard to make time to do all the things for yourself and the people in your life and stay current on what's happening in the world at any given moment.

Most of us are busy making sure everyone is fed and chauffeuring kids from one thing to the other. We have to make sure we eat enough protein and drink enough water, we get our steps in, sleep seven to nine hours every night, and get the laundry folded, all while holding down a job to pay for said activities, food, and life. How could we possibly find the time for one more thing? Even if that one more thing is just taking a few minutes to recognize and be still with God. Some days, it's just too much to be still at all. The demands of life are heavy upon us.

What I am about to say will not surprise you.

We are stretched really thin.

This is not earth-shattering news; it's our cultural reality.

It used to be that we had to keep up with the Joneses who lived next door. But now there's also social media Sallys and Sams, coworker Cathys and soccer club Stephens. We are overwhelmed by the influence of so many others today, be it on our phones that are glued to our hands or in person.

We know in our heads that Jesus is involved in our lives and invites us to live at a different pace than the one we find ourselves running at day in and day out, but walking at that pace is easier said than done.

We want to please God and make wise choices for ourselves and the ones in our care. We are good-hearted people. So why do we often feel as if God is distant? Why is it such a struggle to hear from him and to know exactly what he wants from our lives?

I don't have all the answers, but I am convinced our busyness has something to do with our feelings that there's distance between God and our daily lives. We're busy. From the moment our alarm clock screams at us in the dawn hours until our heavy heads hit the pillow at night, we. Are. Busy. There are demands placed upon us from our spouses, our parents, our toddlers, the kids' school, not to mention church activities, the sports schedule, work deadlines, unread text messages, bills, and financial decisions we need to make. Heaven forbid someone gets sick and we need to become nurse for a loved one in the midst of the chaos. Or worse, *we* get sick but the demands of life don't stop for anyone or anything.

Have you ever felt that God was silent for a season in your life? Maybe he feels distant and uninterested in your life in this moment. It's difficult to surrender to and accept an invitation from a God who feels far off.

There may be other reasons for this, but I am convinced that a large part of feeling like God is distant has something to do with how busy and distracted we find ourselves all too often. At least, that's certainly been the case in my life.

The good news is, we don't have to succumb to the culture's lead. We don't have to keep the hamster-wheel pace and strive to be all the things and do all the things.

Rather, we were made to rely on the One by whom all things were made and in whom all things are held together.

We are free to stop the rat race, slow down, and tune our ears to hear from the living God.

Jesus' way invites us to do as much.

When he walked the earth, living the human experience, Jesus hushed the noise and demands of his life often. I imagine he spent much more time alone and in prayer than we know. And because his way is always better, we can know exactly what to do to close that gap that causes us to feel as if God is distant from us, and we can live life confident of his closeness and care, despite the tornado of life swirling around us constantly.

I want us to look for a moment at an example in the Old Testament that I think we can all relate to when it comes to going through the motions of this Christian life, yet still feeling disconnected from God.

In 1 Samuel 3, we read about a young boy named, you guessed it, Samuel. At this time in history, God wasn't very chatty with folks. Samuel and those around him didn't hear from God often. His voice and his presence among the people were rare. When the chapter opens, Samuel has never heard from God, despite spending most of his young life in the temple.

He grew up in the temple. He served and worked in the temple day in and day out. Surely he would be close to God, right? Certainly, God would see and bless Samuel's service and dedication to all things holy, right? We sometimes have the same thought about all we may be doing in service to the church. Doesn't God see when we volunteer in the kid's ministry once a month? Doesn't he see me doing my Bible study homework and squeezing in my quiet time first thing in the morning? Don't these acts of service for him mean he will bless us and speak to us?

Our lives' busyness absolutely impairs our hearing the Lord *and* our expectations of exactly what we should hear.

We can be confident God bends his ear and listens to our every word.[1] We can also be confident that he speaks to us and fights for us constantly. We see this much and more in this story of Samuel.

One night, Samuel went to bed like every other night. But on this one particular night, as he lay in his bed, he heard someone call his name. Samuel got up and ran to an old man named Eli, the temple priest, thinking it was Eli who had called him. But it wasn't Eli who called Samuel.

Samuel went back to bed and the same thing happened again. He heard someone call him. By this time, I imagine Samuel may have been annoyed. I'd be wondering if old man Eli was messing with me, you know what I mean? I imagine him thinking to himself, *What's a guy got do to get some sleep around here?*

A second time he runs to Eli and, again, Eli tells him he didn't call him and to go back to sleep already. Eli must have been annoyed too.

You're not going to believe this, but the whole scene unfolded a third time. Finally, it dawned on Eli that it was God calling for Samuel. He told Samuel to lie down again and, sure enough, God called Samuel a fourth time.

Here's what the Scripture says happened next, "The LORD came and stood there, calling as at the other times, 'Samuel! Samuel!' Then Samuel said, 'Speak, for your servant is listening.'"[2]

Wow. Can you imagine? The Lord came and stood there and called Samuel by name. I'm pretty sure Samuel was very much awake at this point.

The good Lord knows how to get our attention. He wants to get our attention because he has invitations for us to quiet the chaos around us so that we might experience life abundantly and to the full. He didn't make us to run the rat race and drown in busyness. We were created to flourish in this life, and we won't get to experience his intention for us so long as we're too busy and too distracted to hear his voice and to follow his lead in our lives.

The character of God, the nature of Jesus, and the nearness of the Holy Spirit tell us how much he desires to speak to us and to have us hear him with the ears he fashioned on both sides of our heads.

We were created to hear his voice, know his voice, and respond to his voice.

The world around us is deafeningly loud and constantly working to keep us from hearing and responding to the word of God.

Corrie ten Boom understood this reality. She once said, "If the devil can't make you bad, he'll make you busy."[3]

We want to trust God and live for him. We want to teach our little people about his love. We want to serve others and make a dent of kindness with the time we have on this rapidly spinning globe. We're good people with good hearts. *And* we're busy people.

It's a lot to stay alive, let alone be present with a God we cannot see with our eyes and cannot hear with our ears.

Young Samuel had a terrible role model in old man Eli. Eli spent his days attending to the mundane demands of his temple life. He lit candles and kept temple ordinances. I wonder what he thought about God as he worked and went about his daily duties. I wonder if he questioned whether or not God saw him and was concerned with him, day in and day out.

And then it happened. Unexpectedly, God showed up for Samuel with a message specifically for him that would impact not only Samuel's life but King David's life, Jesus' life, and even our lives today.

God's message for Samuel was the first of many instructions; God would eventually lead him to anoint a young shepherd boy named David as king of Israel. Jesus, the King of all Kings, came from the line of David. And because Jesus died on the cross for our sins and rose again three days later, you and I can know him and live redeemed and restored as God's people.

Tuning our ears to hear the voice of God not only impacts our lives, but has implications for those around us and future generations.

Let that thought soak in like the sun on a summer day at the beach.

God is a deeply personal and relational God who is authoring an everlasting-to-everlasting story and you are part of it. He has a message for you.

He knows your name.

He knows your circumstances.

He knows the deeply rooted desires of your heart.

He knows your thoughts and your hopes and dreams.

He knows your disappointments.

He knows your secrets.

He knows your struggle.

He knows your failures.

He knows what you're really thinking.

And not only does he know these things about you uniquely, he cares for you beyond all measure and comprehension.

John 10:3 says, "The gatekeeper opens the gate for him, and the sheep listen to his voice. He calls his own sheep by name and leads them out."

Jesus knows our names. We were designed to hear his voice and follow his lead. These words are more refreshing and life-giving than an ice-cold sparkling water on a blazing hot summer's day.

God is always active and always up to something good. We have assurance as much throughout his Word.

And God will show up for me and for you like

he did for Samuel and so many others we read about in the Bible. He has a message to give to every one of us.

The presence of God stood before Samuel and he called him by name. In this moment, God invited Samuel into the story of God in the world. I believe God is still calling our names and inviting us into the story that he is telling in the world.

It's the better story for us, for those around us, and for the ones who will come after us.

So how do we resist the busyness and hear his voice?

I think we simply ask him to tune our ears to his voice, and then we create space for him to speak and for us to listen. Practically, this will look a little different for each one of us. If the phone is your distraction, try turning your notifications off or putting parameters around when you'll use your phone throughout the day. Maybe you turn it off between the hours of seven p.m. and seven a.m.

Maybe you pass on summer sports for the kids and take a break from the demands sports can place on a family and, instead, use the time to connect more with them as a family.

Maybe you say no this quarter to serving at your church so that you can be served and fill your tank up again, so that in the next season, you can serve in a healthier manner.

Maybe you spend just ten minutes every morning recognizing the air in your lungs that Jesus has given you, and ask him to speak to you in that moment and throughout the day.

Maybe instead of scrolling on social media, you take a walk with ears open to what he might have for you at that time.

Maybe instead of blasting Journey through your car speakers on your commute, you drive in silence and listen for the voice of God in your car. (That one is for me.)

Jesus doesn't operate out of busyness like we do. He has a better way. He is the better way. We'll look more closely at this in a later chapter.

Jesus doesn't ask us to do one more thing in life to serve him. Rather, his desire is to be near and to be infused into every area of our life, from laundry to carpool to chaotic family dinners and everything in between.

Jesus isn't just one more person we have to worry about pleasing. He doesn't expect us to be busy for him. He simply wants to be near us and to help guide us through the crazy.

He knows your name. He knows the demands

of life placed upon you. He stands before you with arms stretched wide, and invites you to allow him to help you navigate your way.

Speak, Lord; your servants are listening.

Jesus invites us to hear the whisper of his voice in our lives.

CHAPTER 3

Invited to Lose Control

My black 1998 4Runner spun completely around three times across three lanes of the highway before coming to a complete stop on the right-hand shoulder.

The loss of control left me no other choice but to cry out to Jesus and beg him to literally take the wheel.

Three lanes of fast-moving traffic had come to a full stop, and they stayed that way until it was evident that I had too. Then they began to drive off, leaving me and my racing heart at the side of the road.

A concerned driver pulled over behind me and, with trepidation, approached my driver's side window. I rolled the window down as he stared intently at me and then scanned the back seat. "Are you okay? Is there anyone else in the car with you?"

After I assured him that I was shaken up but completely fine and no one else was in the car with me, he smiled and said, "Well then I have to tell you, that was the coolest spinout I have ever seen!"

Nobody likes the idea of a spinout, be it a literal spinout like mine or an emotional spinout, swirling around and wondering how and when it will end.

Somewhere along the line, I realized I really liked the idea that I'm in control. I'm guessing you're with me in this.

I like to think that I can manipulate and control outcomes by my own behavior—including the times I use my own behavior to influence the behavior of others, like my husband or sons.

It's why flying sometimes makes me anxious: because for the duration of the trip, from takeoff to landing, I have no choice but to rely on the pilots, whom I cannot see or talk to. That doesn't exactly make me feel safe and secure like my false sense of control does.

Safe and secure.

These are two *s* words that have a great impact

on you and me. We need to feel safe and secure. Our desire for safety and security is part of how we were wired from the very beginning, and it's actually a sign of our dependence. Adam and Eve were completely dependent upon God before sin entered the world and gave them the false notion that they could create their own safety net apart from him and manufacture their own security without his help.

We also tend toward believing—and therefore living as if—we are in control and independent of God. When we are left feeling unsafe and not at all secure, we still try to manufacture safety and security for ourselves and for the ones we love.

I'm not exactly proud to admit this, but, my friend, I do this all the time. It's probably why I do most of the driving when we're in the car as a family. I just take the wheel without a second thought. My husband, the Pilot, doesn't argue. He simply gets into the passenger seat, and I imagine the eyes of his mind roll in his head, but he doesn't say a word about it ever. He lets me have my false sense of security and control as I drive the family down the road.

But the reality is that he's a fantastic driver. He's cautious and aware of his surroundings. He's never had a ticket nor been in an accident. Me, on the other hand? I've had plenty of speeding tickets, an illegal left turn ticket, and a few minor fender benders. But who's counting?

Despite the overwhelming evidence, I still feel like I need to be the one in control of the wheel.

Is there an area in your life where, despite the contrary evidence, you consider yourself in control?

Perhaps a better way to phrase that question is to ask, Where in your life do you have room to grow in dependence upon Jesus? Where do you *need to lose the need* to be in control in order to see and to know that only Jesus is in control and has authority over all things?

When we take control, one, we're not actually really in control of anything, so we set ourselves up to be very disappointed when outcomes don't work out like we think they should. And two, we mislead others to falsely believe they can depend on us for their wellbeing, when, in fact, we disappoint each other time and time again.

I'm a work in progress of course, but more and more, I am learning to be okay with not being the one in control (I never thought I'd say those words). Instead, I'm beginning to relish the freedom and peace that surrounds me when I remember that it is Jesus and only Jesus who is in control. And herein lies the safest, most secure place we could ever find ourselves.

Only he is able to give you and me safety and security. This is his design for us, and it's the better way to live—for us and for those around us, beginning in our own household.

The Scriptures tell us that Jesus holds all things together.[1] *All things*, meaning everything from the positioning of the stars in the sky down to the exact place you live.

He revealed just how much he is in control of all things when he walked the earth alongside humanity. He restored sight to the blind, hearing to the deaf, and words to the mute. He walked on water and calmed the raging sea. And he raised the dead to life.

Jesus invites us to loosen our grip on our need for control so that our hands may be free to experience and hold on to the peace and freedom that come from knowing and trusting that he is in control and all we need.

I want us to look at just one example in Scripture where Jesus revealed just how little control we have in this world, and how limitless are his authority and control.

In John 11, we read the remarkable story of one particular household. It was made up of three siblings who were friends of Jesus: sisters Mary and Martha, and their brother, Lazarus.

Jesus was in a distant land when he heard news that Lazarus was sick. It sounded serious, but Jesus didn't rush off to help. Instead, he said some strange things about Lazarus being asleep and then went on about his day.

By this time, the disciples had spent enough time with Jesus to know he was able to heal and restore, so I imagine they were confused as to why Jesus didn't go immediately to Lazarus to heal him. After all, Jesus and Lazarus were good friends. If Jesus had healed strangers, wouldn't he also heal those close to him?

How often do we think along the same lines? How often do our conversations with Jesus involve lots of questions about why our circumstances aren't panning out the way we would like them to or think would be best? We know he's capable of fixing this situation to our liking or restoring that estranged relationship, so why doesn't he? We believe he can heal our illness or the illness of a loved one, but why doesn't he? We're confident he is in control of all things, so why does life feel so very out of control?

The disciples expected Jesus to react to hearing the news about his friend by quickly moving to heal Lazarus. But that's not at all what Jesus did. If we zoom out a little bit, we'll be better able to see that Jesus had a far greater plan for healing than what the disciples could see and understand in the moment. He was in more control over Lazarus' sickness and life than was visible to the disciples.

And the same is true of you and me today. Let that sink in for a minute.

Our lives are in the hands of the one who knew our names and our unique quirks before he laid the foundations of the earth. Our lives are in the hands of the one who formed us in our mom's tummy before we took our first breath. He is the one who sees all things, knows all things, and literally holds all things together, today, tomorrow, and forever.

You know how the story ends. Jesus told Lazarus to walk out of the grave and he did. And God was glorified because this whole scene of events was part of his story.

He is writing your story. He has your life in the palm of his hand. You can take a deep breath and find all you need for today and every day in him.

This story shows us that there is nothing we cannot depend upon Jesus for. Even when life is coming undone at the seams and we don't feel safe and secure and we find ourselves grasping for control in order to change the outcome, there we find Jesus graciously rescuing, restoring, renewing, and giving life.

When we zoom out a bit in our lives, as we just did in looking at the story of Lazarus, we will become more and more prone to yield to Jesus' control and depend upon him instead of ourselves. As we grow in our faith and trust in him, this practice of depending upon him before ourselves will strengthen us. In time, we will learn to loosen our grip upon the false idea that we know what's best and can control anything on any given day.

Jesus invites us to fully rely upon him and his words of truth. He invites us to live a life where we constantly loosen our grip on the things we don't actually have in our hands to begin with, in order to cling tighter to him.

We must lose our need to be in control of ourselves in order to gain confidence in Christ.

A mysterious and glorious exchange takes place along the path walked towards giving up our need to be in control of our lives. As we walk in step with Jesus and grow our trust in him and his abilities and authority in our lives, our need for self-reliance will fade. In its place, the Holy Spirit creates in us the ability to exercise self-control. Jesus invites us to give up our need to be in control and instead to rely, not on ourselves, but on him and him alone.

He invites us to trust him, even in the depths of great grief or confusion, when all hope feels lost. What a kind and gracious gift given to us by our creator!

Giving up the need for control is not a one and done. Instead, it's a daily act of surrender. Okay, let's be honest here: some days it's a minute-by-minute practice! That's what it takes to give up any sense of control we believe we have and to yield to the only one who has real authority and control over our very breath and life.

The sinful nature we were born with causes us to believe we are in control. Without so much as a second thought, we work hard to tighten our grip and attempt to hold all things together in our lives by our own strength. But we will quickly discover just how not in control we really are. And for a control freak like me, the feeling of losing control can be a scary thing.

Just moments before my highway spinout, I was cruising along, living my best false-sense-of-control life without a care in the world, and within a nanosecond, I was completely out of control.

Any sense that we may have of being in control of outcomes is false and like standing on sinking sand, expecting it to hold us up.

I wonder if Jesus' disciples felt that they too were in control and had this following Jesus thing figured out—at least until he didn't do or say what they expected him to do and say, challenging their perspective and what they thought they knew. By the time these events with Lazarus took place, they had been with Jesus for a few years. They may have felt they had him figured out, which would explain their shock and confusion when Jesus didn't run to heal his friend like they expected he would.

Instead of reacting to circumstances the way we do when we believe we are in control, and wasting no time getting to Lazarus, Jesus waited four days before he went to his friend. Four whole, long days. Obviously, by this time, Lazarus was dead. Three days dead, in fact. That's code for dead, dead, like really dead. Imagine how much more confused the disciples must have felt when the already dire circumstances seemed to get a lot worse.

But Jesus didn't leave them without explanation, and that explanation is also an explanation for the why question of our own unfavorable circumstances today. It's the answer to why things don't pan out the way we often want them to or think they should.

When Jesus first learned of Lazarus' sickness, he said his sickness would not end in death. How confusing for his disciples when Lazarus then died! I wonder if they doubted Jesus and all they had witnessed him say and do up to this moment?

But he continued, "No, it is for God's glory so that God's Son may be glorified through it."[2]

Jesus is about the business of God. He and the Holy Spirit forever work together to accomplish the purpose and plan they established long before the creation of the world and before you and I came along.

God has been authoring a story from everlasting to everlasting. He does not change his story or his plan based on our circumstances. Rather, our circumstances are merely a snippet of his greater story.

He has already written every second of every

day that ever will be. When we accept his invitation to allow him to truly be the master and authority in our lives, we are freed to live how he designed us to: with peace, freedom, and those two *s* words we desperately need, *safety* and *security*.

It's hard to remember this comforting truth in the midst of great grief and disappointment over unmet expectations. When Jesus showed up at Mary and Martha's house, they didn't hold back in giving Jesus a piece of their minds. At different times, they both declared to Jesus, "If you had been here, my brother would not have died."[3]

The sisters believed Jesus could have saved their brother had he only been there for them. Jesus was about to blow their mind with just how real his healing power and authority over all things and all peoples is. He was about to show them that he does all things for the glory of the Father and the good of his children. Jesus was going to show Martha and Mary and all the spectators witnessing these events that he could be trusted with their lives.

In John 11:25, Jesus responded to Martha with an invitation. With these words, Jesus invited Martha to loosen her grip on any false sense of control she might have felt in the moment and, rather, to trust him and find her dependence solely upon him: "I am the resurrection and the life. The one who believes in me will live, even though they die."[4]

He invited Martha and Mary to trust the story that he was writing and to put their full hope and dependence upon him.

And his invitation stands for you and me today.

If Jesus is *the resurrection and the life*, then there is nothing we cannot fully and completely depend upon him for.

During what clearly must have been a chaotic and confusing time for Mary and Martha, Jesus showed us that it's okay for us to not be in control. He certainly doesn't expect perfect mastery from us. He created us and knows we're simply not *built* to be in control. We need only to depend on him.

Despite the deep temporary pain his dear friends felt in this story, the truth he revealed about who he is made it all worth it. The same is true for us as we experience for ourselves the freedom that comes from restored dependence for all things in our lives, even life itself.

I certainly have a ways to go in learning to loosen my white-knuckle grip on so many areas of my life. But I believe Jesus has proven over and over that his way is better and he can be trusted in and with all things you or I will ever experience in our lifetimes.

Consider this your official permission to lose control, dear reader and friend. Find your safety and security in him alone and allow him to give you his peace.

There is freedom to be found in letting go and anchoring ourselves to whatever Jesus has planned for us. There is peace to experience when we follow his lead.

Jesus invites us to loosen our grip on any false sense of self-reliant control, so that we might hold tighter to and depend fully upon him.

CHAPTER 4

Invited to Live the Better Way

I'll never forget the Sunday I met Kelly.

I have, however, forgotten if her name was indeed Kelly. It's been a minute since we met, and I tend to forget most things quicker than two shakes of a lamb's tail.

I served as the outreach director at a church in Huntington Beach, California. It was as rough as it sounds. Huntington Beach, California, has beautiful weather year-round, is known as Surf City, and there you can find great fish tacos on every corner. You could say it's an alright place, and by *alright*, please hear me say it is *fantastic*.

I was inside the lobby of the church, chatting it up with friends, when someone came to me to let me know a young lady was outside, and she wanted to talk to someone on staff. I made my way through the doors of the church and onto the front patio, where I found a tall, beautiful woman in her early twenties with gorgeous brown hair and ripped arms. She was really fit. I would soon learn she was a rescue/fire lifeguard for LA County Fire & Rescue. And then her biceps made sense.

Kelly and I sat down on a large circular concrete planter that served as homebase to a tall southern California palm tree. And that's when Kelly, seated beside me, opened her Bible to the book of Acts and asked me, "Have you read the book of Acts?" Her simple question caught me off guard. As the outreach director, I was a little more accustomed to being asked for food, hygiene supplies, or help with bills.

Her unusual question caused me to chuckle a little, mostly because I had no idea where her question was headed. "Yes, Kelly, I've read the book of Acts." Kelly looked down at the pages of her opened Bible and she began to weep. Her face leaked all over the pages and, struggling to speak through the sobs, she told me a story of how she'd never known God before, but through the stories in Acts, she saw that he clearly knew her.

Kelly shared story after story of how God

spoke directly to her through the book of Acts. Some of what she experienced and faced as a lifeguard and avid ocean swimmer synced up well with the names, people, and places she read about in Acts, even down to the name of the town where she and a fellow swimmer were in a dangerous situation in northern California, wondering if they would survive. The town? Fairhaven. Paul's journey led him by ship to Fair Havens, Crete.

As Kelly shared stories from the book of Acts that resonated profoundly in her personal life, she asked me repeatedly, "Have you read this? Did you know this?" Kelly was absolutely amazed by God's Word and how clearly God used it to speak directly into her life. God shared his deep love for Kelly through his Word—specifically, Acts—and she was genuinely awed.

Kelly reminded me just how alive God's Word is.

The author of Hebrews says as much: "For the word of God is alive and active."[1]

I have to admit I forget this truth often.

It's far too easy to read the Bible because we know we should and forget how utterly dependent we are upon the life-giving truth it speaks right into the depths of our souls.

Have you ever felt like the Bible was speaking directly to you and the circumstances of your life like Kelly did?

It's amazing to stop and consider how this ancient text written by numerous authors over the span of many years and written to a variety of audiences continues to speak to you and me today. Each of us is in a different context. Some of us live in big cities and are accustomed to the constant sound of sirens and cars honking. Others may live in more remote areas, where our own thoughts are the loudest noises we hear.

And yet, the Bible speaks a message for every single person on this green earth, no matter what our zip code is, because all people were designed to hear from God. It's part of how he made us from the very beginning. God walked and talked directly with Adam and Eve before sin gave humanity a hearing problem.

Our hearing is impaired and we no longer walk and talk with God the way the first man and woman did in Eden, but in his mercy and grace, God gave us his Word, so that we might know him, despite the sin that separated God and man. We could no longer go to him, so he came to us.

His Word has the power to change us. As Paul

reminded a young Timothy, "All Scripture is God-breathed and is useful for teaching, rebuking, correcting and training in righteousness."[2]

There's a scandalous story told in the book of John. Jesus walked out of his way to have a conversation with a woman who worked really hard to avoid talking with others.

We don't know the woman's background, but Jesus did and we know she was living her ordinary life and going about her typical daily business when he showed up and changed her life with a few simple words.

And here's the thing: His desire to change our lives today, with his word, remains.

No doubt this unnamed woman was carrying out her normal routines and responding to the demands of her day. She may have been going through the motions of life, the same kind of motions we all know too well. She was minding her own business when, by the word and presence of Jesus, she was changed forever. Not only was she changed forever; her entire town was changed.

You may be familiar with the story of the woman at the well. I prefer to call her the woman of the word because, like Kelly, it was the words of Jesus that changed her. And not only that, it was the words of her testimony about what Jesus had said to her, when he told her everything she had ever done, that led her entire town to the life-giving words of Jesus.

You can read about this story in John 4.

There are so many reasons she should've never talked with Jesus that afternoon, but Jesus had other plans and another purpose for this woman, and he used his words to change everything for her and her neighbors. This women at the well thought she was going to draw water for the day, but then Jesus talked about living water and how, in him, she would never thirst again.

His invitation to hear his word and to receive the living water which will cause us to never thirst again still stands.

Where in your life are you thirsty for more? Do you have desert lands in your life that you wish the floodgates would open up upon? Do you feel stuck in the mundane of day-to-day tasks and responsibilities and long for peace and joy? Are you lacking purpose, and are you thirsty for fullness?

Jesus has words for you, friend. They are words to fill you up where you are empty and words to give life where you feel defeated.

His invitation to the woman at the well was to

receive eternal life. This is the living water that he spoke of. Eternal life begins the moment we believe and receive Jesus and take him at his word that he is the Christ—he is the rescue, the redemption, and the salvation we desperately need.

Kelly remains the only person I've ever met who literally wept over the pages of her Bible in response to the love of God for her written all over its pages.

I later learned that Kelly hadn't grown up in the church and hadn't spent any time with Christians. She was completely unfamiliar with the story of God and his created design and way for his people. But she was eager to learn and strongly desired to live her life reflective of God and his ways because she so clearly saw that God saw her and offered her living water and eternal life so that she might not thirst again, and he did it by his Word.

What Kelly was experiencing as she read Acts was the discovery of a better way to live. She was glorious shocked by the God who could meet her so specifically through stories written a very long time ago. She craved knowledge of God and had an intense desire to live in the way he designed. She longed to give up trying to forge her own way and, rather, wanted to yield to God's way and Word because it was so clear he was speaking directly to her through the tear-stained pages.

She tasted his sovereignty and goodness and decided it was better than anything she could create for herself apart from God. She was in the process of choosing his way and foregoing her own.

The fact that Jesus' words give eternal life are all the nudge we need to crack open our Bibles and expectantly read the literal Word of God. God loves you so deeply that he sent his one and only Son, Jesus, who willingly stooped to our lowly, deprived, sinful world to be near us. God came to us first in the person of Jesus and is now even closer by the Spirit who dwells within us from the moment we believe and receive him.

The love of God may feel too good to be true, especially in light of our rotting conditions caused by sin. And because of the mercy and kindness of Christ, the small stories we can tell on our own aren't the end. They weren't the end for the woman at the well and they certainly aren't the end of your story or mine.

The story God is writing is far bigger and wider and more complete than we can ever imagine. We will never fully comprehend the endless love of Christ. And that's okay. We don't need to understand in order to receive.

He simply invites us to know him through his Word and to live according to his way. He has living water for each of us. His well will never run dry. Those unfulfilled areas of your life? Try drinking in his Word and watch him fill you up.

There's a short story in the Bible about another woman who momentarily forgot the word of God and it changed the course of history.

Remember Eve? The sly serpent caused her to doubt God's word when he asked her, "Did God really say, 'You must not eat from any tree in the garden?'"[3] Not only did he use his words to twist God's, he caused her to wonder if she had heard God correctly.

Sound familiar? How often do we feel confused by the Word or doubt the truth of God's Word? It's the same lie on repeat. Satan is boring and not at all creative. He's still using the same tactics on us—tactics designed to trip us up so that we miss out on the fullness of life that knowing God's Word and obeying his truth yields.

As a result of their sin and disobedience to God, Eve and her man, Adam, had to leave the garden. This meant they could no longer be near God and hear his every word spoken to them directly during their daily garden strolls.

But for those of us who know Christ as Savior, we simply need to use our words to voice when we're offtrack. The Spirit within us will guide us back to Jesus' word and way. And he'll lead us back to Christ no matter how many times we stray.

The woman at the well arrived at the well not only with an empty water jug; she was also physically and emotionally empty. No amount of well water would change her life or pick up the broken pieces and bring her any consolation or resolution. But Jesus' word was the living water. It was what her thirsty soul truly longed for and needed.

Friend, his invitation for us to be changed by his word still stands. It wasn't just for the woman at the well. It isn't just for ripped-arm Kelly. His invitation extends to you too. It's available today and again tomorrow and the next day after that. His water never runs dry. We're invited to drink from the well of his words daily.

We're invited to hear rightly again the words of our Creator. We're invited to drink living water and never thirst again. Our Bibles speak the name of the risen Christ on every page.

Kelly is the only person I've ever seen express so much emotion and shed so many tears as she realized the God of the Scriptures knows her so deeply and intimately. She was changed by her encounter with the living Word.

The woman at the well was changed too, and the change didn't stop with her. Her entire village also came to believe in Jesus as a result of her testimony of meeting and talking with Jesus at the well that day.

The author of Psalm 119 captures so beautifully the longing in our hearts to remain in the Word and tethered to the source of everything good in our lives. Take a minute to reflect and pray through these verses.

> How can a young person stay on the path
>   of purity?
>   By living according to your word.
> I seek you with all my heart;
>   do not let me stray from your commands.
> I have hidden your word in my heart
>   that I might not sin against you.

Praise be to you, LORD;
> teach me your decrees.
With my lips I recount
> all the laws that come from your mouth.
I rejoice in following your statutes
> as one rejoices in great riches.
I meditate on your precepts
> and consider your ways.
I delight in your decrees;
> I will not neglect your word.[4]

May you find fullness as you spend time in the presence of Jesus, filling up on his life-giving words.

Jesus invites us to drink his Words of living water every day.

CHAPTER 5

Invited to Walk and Talk with Jesus

There is no safer place to be than by the side of our good and kind creator, Jesus.

Where he is, is the very place we were designed to be, forever and always.

I haven't always felt near to Jesus, but he has certainly been close to me, despite how I might have felt.

I'm certain I'm not alone in this experience and that you've had your moments or seasons where you also felt distance between yourself and Jesus.

Like you, I've had many seasons and many occasions when I've wondered if Jesus was near, and I've wandered in my doubt.

It's one thing to believe Jesus cares about our lives as a whole—that he cares about the big stuff we may be going through—but what about the more detailed and mundane parts of our lives? Does Jesus still care as much about our life's circumstances when it comes to our day-to-day thoughts, feelings, and actions?

The short answer is a resounding *yes*. But I think this is where we can get tripped up so easily. We know Jesus cares, but all too often, we feel as if the details of our daily life are not important enough to bother Jesus with. After all, a lot of people are dealing with way bigger situations, so it doesn't feel right to even talk with him about the stuff in our lives.

If you're like me, you feel very grateful for all you have. So, if we dared to start talking to Jesus about the longings in our hearts, wouldn't we just be exposing how needy we truly are?

Maybe we're really great at getting up before the sun to spend a few minutes in prayer and in the Word, only to lose sight of Jesus as yet another busy day unfolds and we find ourselves in high demand. We forget our need for him because we're knee-deep in caring for the needs of our families and our coworkers.

If any of these scenarios resonates with you, friend, you are in good company. If we're honest, we all feel this way a lot throughout life. If you're in a season of doubt, be encouraged that you won't remain there. Jesus cares too deeply for you to keep you in that state. He's actively growing you as you walk the road of doubt. Remain close to him and share your heart with him. In time, he will help you understand the season you're in and you'll be stronger in your faith because of the precious time you spent with him.

Not too long ago, I was upset about how things were going in my life. My health wasn't where I wanted it to be. My time wasn't allocated how I wanted it to be. I felt unclear regarding next steps in my creative pursuits. And for several days I journaled about my frustration. I stewed over all that wasn't going my way, and after some time of this, I was really at a loss for how to get out of the funk I found myself buried beneath.

It was during this time of feeling completely helpless and unsure of how to even begin to make some much-needed changes in my life that I went on a walk. The J Men were on their bikes just ahead of me, and I poured my heart out to Jesus. With raw and honest emotion, I told him exactly what I was thinking, even if it sounded dumb to say out loud. I told him the emotions I had swirling about in my heart, even if they made me sound ungrateful. And I expressed how I was feeling, even if I sounded selfish in doing so.

Have you ever vented to Jesus before? Maybe you've been on a walk-and-talk vent session with Jesus, like I was on that December day. Maybe you were in your car or at the park. It's so good for our souls to talk all things out with Jesus, who is the only one who can rightly listen and respond.

He's the best listener ever (after all, he created the ear and hearing, so he can be trusted to hear when we speak). And his response will always be exactly what we need and come when we need it (spend some time in the Psalms and you'll soon discover these truths for yourself).

Regardless of what we unload onto Jesus, he's never unconcerned with what we have to say or too busy to be present with us and lean in to listen. I think that sentence should be read again, so here it goes: *Regardless of what we unload onto Jesus, he's never unconcerned with what we have to say or too busy to be present with us and lean in to listen.*

We have his Word that declares over and over again the depth of his compassionate care for us and the truth that he is continuously, unconditionally available. Not only is he available and a good listener, Jesus desires to be involved in every part of our lives. Yes, the big and the small stuff. If he cared enough to endure the cross for us, then I think it's safe to say there is no one who loves us more than he does.

Back to my vent-session walk with Jesus. Somewhere along the way, and in the middle of unloading all I was thinking and feeling, I heard the gentle but firm whisper of the Spirit. *Carrie, walk with me.*

I walked further and thought, *Walk with you? What does that mean? Like I'm walking with my kids now? I would love it if I could really walk with you, Jesus.*

And then I heard it again. *Walk with me, Carrie.*

There it was. Another invitation from Jesus: the invitation to walk with him.

The angst I had been experiencing subsided with a surrendered exhale and a silent acknowledgment that Jesus was present, he had heard my cry, and because he was near, I could calm my soul and find the rest I needed.

Of course, my immediate question back was, *Okay, but what exactly does that mean, Jesus?* I wanted specifics, as I'm sure you do too when you consider what it means for you to walk with Jesus.

Did Jesus mean I ought to continue literally going on these types of walks and talks with him? Was it because he knew that my thighs were conjoined twins that needed to be separated and gain their independence once again?

That could be the case, but knowing Jesus, there must be a little more to the invitation to walk with him than mere exercise.

John, a friend of Jesus, wrote of walking with God. We read about it in a handcrafted letter to his friend Gaius: "I have no greater joy than to hear that my children are walking in the truth."[1]

What did John mean, "walking in the truth"?

I think walking in the truth is walking with God, and this walking is illustrated in several ways in our lives. These are just a few of the ways I've discovered of what it looks like to walk with God:

- to know deep in the soul that he is who he says he is and can be trusted
- to recognize and believe his Word and the promises that he is near at all times
- to be cognizant of his involvement in our lives and his endless care and compassion

cascading over our lives at all times
- to mimic how Jesus lived and loved as we go about interacting with family, friends, coworkers, etc.
- to talk openly with Jesus, believing he willingly bends his ear towards us and hangs on our every word

What would you add to the list? Have you heard his invitation to walk with him? How did you respond? I wish I could meet up for coffee with you. I could buy you a latte, and you could share all you've experienced in your journey walking with Jesus. I have so much to learn.

At the end of the day, I believe walking with Jesus looks like being aware of his presence throughout the day. No matter how big or small our life's circumstances and situations are, and regardless of where we physically find ourselves, Jesus wants to walk with us, shoulder to shoulder, every day of our lives.

And not only does he want to be near to us, he also wants to be an active participant in our daily lives. He's not passive, orchestrating life's events from afar, as if our lives are merely another note to be played in the grand music hall of life.

Scripture has shown us over and over how personal, intimate, ever present and a constant defender of his people he has been. And the author of Hebrews reminds us that he is "the same yesterday and today and forever."[2] Therefore, we can know he desires to be involved in every detail, big or small, of our lives.

He's nearer than we can imagine.

Even more amazing, he wants to walk beside us! He isn't distant. He's the God who created all things out of love for all things. He's the God who spent the seventh day of creation with the one made in his image. He's the God who is near and loves to walk *with* his people. We see this proven in Eden and we see it time and time again throughout the Old Testament stories. God spoke to Noah, appeared to Abraham, met with Moses, descended upon mountains as a cloud and a pillar of fire, and came to his people in a tent and in a temple.

And then after a period of nearly five hundred years without God's physical presence nearby and right when it must have seemed as though all hope that God would come near his people again was lost, Jesus entered the human story as a baby born in a manger. In the dark night, light had come. The dawn of a new day arrived; hope for God's people was renewed when baby Jesus was born and life changed for all eternity.

What must Mary and Joseph have felt as they held their creator in their arms? But even with this reach of God towards us again, he wasn't done showing his people just how near he desired to be or just how much he desired to walk with us on the journey of life.

On the other side of the resurrection, Christ ascended and gave his people the gift of his presence once again. But this time—his love being so great for his people and his desire to be near so strong—his presence would take up residence *inside* his people.

All people, including you and me, no longer have to physically go where he is, as if he could be contained in one place. We do not need to travel to a distant land to be near our God. We don't have to visit a church building to hear from him. We don't have to speak through a pastor or priest in order for him to hear what's on our minds and the stirring in our hearts. He is wherever we are because he has made his dwelling within us.

He has taken up residence in our soul. You can't get nearer to a person than in their guts.

"See what great love the Father has lavished on us, that we should be called children of God! And that is what we are!"[3]

So long as you have air in your lungs, the invitation to walk with him stands. There is always opportunity to say yes to walking with him and to grow in trust of him with each step forward. We can grow in our ability to be cognizant of him outside of quiet times. His invitation to us to be constantly aware of his presence and place in our life always stands.

We can grow in learning to walk with him daily. He's a God who desires to be known. He invites us to know him. He's a God who loves adventure and play and joy. And he invites us to adventure—to play and experience joy alongside him. He is a God who despises sin and therefore invites us to accept his gift of salvation, a rescue from the bondage of sin—a rescue we are so desperately in need of. He is a good and holy God, and, therefore, he invites us to trust him. He's all-powerful and all-knowing, and he invites us to rest under the wings of his authority and might.

When we feel overwhelmed by the chaos swirling around us, he invites us to find our peace in him alone.

When we're helpless, he is where our help comes from.

When we're tired, he invites us to go to him and rest.

When we're weak, he invites us to draw from his unending strength.

And when we're overcome by grief, he invites us to receive his comfort.

Jesus is the way. He's the path towards home. He's the clearly marked path, leading the way towards the place we were designed to be: in the presence of the good and loving God who made us out of his abundant love for us.

All my angst about the unwanted areas of my life subsided when I heard and received the invitation to walk with Jesus.

My circumstances didn't change. I still have many areas of life that are not at all what I want them to be (I'm looking at you, thigh twins). But walking with Jesus has meant that I talk it out with him more regularly, and when he speaks, I'm more and more mindful to listen and more likely to trust and obey.

The outcome isn't an Instagram-worthy life. Rather, it's something much greater. Friend, we do not walk this road of life alone, left to figure out all the things—the big, the small, and everything in between—on our own. There is nothing so small, so insignificant, so unimportant that Jesus won't show up for you there, in your time of need.

There are many days my kids are so excited to show me or tell me something. And almost always, I'm up to my green eyeballs in something when they come calling. I'm not perfect at it, but I sure try to stop what I'm doing so that I can be present with them, watch them, or listen to them show me whatever it is. I want them to know I care about what they're doing and what they have to say to me. Of course I have my moments, but I try to let it be known that, as their mom, I love it when they share things with me, no matter what it may be. There is nothing too small or too unimportant for me to pay attention to when they call and ask me about it.

I'm excited and amazed when they share their latest LEGO builds with me. I love watching them make volcanoes with baking soda and vinegar in the yard. I love hearing about their days when I pick them up from school. (Yes, they're still young enough that I get a fair amount of info and insight about what's going down at school. I know these days are fleeting.)

I typically don't mind when the J Men interrupt me to share something with me, because, as their mom, I care so deeply for them. I want to know what they're thinking, doing, and feeling.

I'm sure you feel the same with loved ones in your circle.

So how much more, then, does Jesus care for you?

Jesus' invitation to walk with him is for all of us. He invites us to recognize him day by day, moment by moment. He wants us to simply be cognizant that he's in the room. He is near, regardless of where we find ourselves, in the wide-open spaces to the hidden places.

"I'm here. I've fully available to you right now. Not after you have your act together or take care of some business. No, right now, no matter what. I care for you and I am with you."

He's constantly inviting us to trust him, follow him, hope in him, heal in him, thank him, praise him, draw near to him. A surrendered life is a life that accepts his daily invitation to walk with him.

Jesus invites us to walk with him in all things, every day of our lives.

CHAPTER 6

Invited to Cast Your Cares

Not long ago, my sons learned how to cast a fishing line.

They explained to me that casting requires them to place the fishing pole well behind and over their shoulders. Once it's fully extended back, with all their might, they hurl the line forward, casting it out as far as their strength can muster, until the hooked line drops into the water beyond the shoreline.

Peter, a disciple of Jesus, wrote about casting. As a fisherman, he understood what it meant to cast. His livelihood depended upon his casting skills. If he didn't cast his nets just right, he wouldn't bring in enough fish to sustain himself and his family.

But when we read Peter's words about casting, he's talking about prayer, not fish. He writes, "Cast all your anxiety on him because he cares for you."[1]

When I consider how my sons were taught to cast their fishing-pole lines into the waters before them, I am struck by the vast difference between their fishing and my praying.

How often do we tend to hold on too tightly to matters we were not built to bear, when Christ so graciously has made a way for us to cast all that's in our hearts upon him?

How might our willingness to truly cast our cares up and over our shoulders and onto the risen Lord Jesus free us up to receive the fullness he has designed for us?

Ultimately, these questions are undergirded by the real question: Do we fully trust him to catch our anxiety, our cares, and the troubles of our hearts? And even if he can catch them, do we trust him to know what to do with them and how to help us in return?

These questions are no surprise to Jesus. He understands us fully and he would've felt the same temptation to keep matters on his heart to himself, but he is not like us and he didn't do that. We read over and over again throughout the gospel books of Jesus spending time alone with the Father. He made it a habit to talk with God often. He's given us such an example of a better way to live—a way that leads to him and his ability to see us through any circumstance we may ever face in this life.

It's no secret that anxiety is felt across cultures and has become painfully prevalent throughout our world in recent years. Concerns for safety of self and loved ones are commonly felt around the globe. Concerns for health, well-being, and financial security are also among the top burdens carried in today's world.

Issues such as the global pandemic of 2020, political unrest, and wars and rumors of wars only add to and compound the concerns and worries of individuals.

We were not designed to know everything going on in the world at any given moment.

We were not built to carry the weight pressed upon our shoulders by these colossal matters.

Remember that Peter understood what it meant to cast. His living depended on how well he cast his nets into the sea. He knew where to cast and at what time of day in order to have the best outcome for a good day's catch.

Peter understood that to cast meant to throw with all his might and to loosen his grip on the net as he fully launched it from the boat. Do we cast our cares on Jesus with the same gumption? Do we use all our might to free ourselves from the weight that presses us down?

It's a common human struggle to hold on to and not fully let go of what's on our minds, the things keeping us awake at night. We wrestle with the question of whether a carefree life is really possible, despite our faith in Jesus. How could we possibly be free from worry and anxiety when we're constantly surrounded by unsettling news, shocking events, and what feels like endless unknowns?

I believe the help we desperately need is revealed to us in the latter part of Peter's words: "He cares for you."

We can be just as confident that Peter knew what he was talking about when he penned those words as we can be that he was an expert fisherman. Why? Because fisherman Peter was a direct, in-the-flesh recipient of the overwhelming, gracious love of Jesus, and it changed everything for him.

If we navigate in our Bibles to John 21, we gain insight into a pivotal, life-changing, and restorative moment in Peter's life.

As the story begins, we find Peter and friends in a boat in the darkness of night and overwhelmed by grief, confusion, and sorrow. After Jesus died, Peter and friends went right back to where they were comfortable and what they were comfortable with. You guessed it, they went fishing.

However, after having not caught a single fish, likely only deepening their pain, they saw the dawn break. The sunlight began to rise along the eastern horizon, and a man called out to them from the shore. He told them to cast their net out one more time.

With what must have been defeated exhaustion, Peter didn't argue and, once again, he cast the net off the side of the boat. But this catch was different. Immediately, the net filled with fish, and in that moment, Peter knew the man on the shore was the risen Lord Jesus.

Jesus met Peter right where he was: knee-deep in his grief. Peter had left everything to follow Jesus. His hope for a better way of life and a better future for his family was completely wrapped up in his belief that Jesus was the Messiah. This same Peter who walked on water by his faith in Jesus. He later witnessed Jesus die on the cross, and a little part of Peter must have felt like it died too.

But then, Jesus demonstrated his great love for Peter by telling him to cast out his net once more.

Are you tired of the weight you carry? Are you drowning in grief? Overwhelmed? Are you unsure of what your next move might be or how best to resolve a situation you face? This is the time to cast your cares upon Jesus. He is just as willing to demonstrate his great love for you today as he was for Peter then.

When we've lost hope and feel as if we're at the end of ourselves and our means, there we find Jesus, arms stretched out wide, ready and expecting to receive all of who we are.

Upon realizing the man on shore was Jesus, Peter leapt out of the boat and swam his way to the shore. He couldn't get to Jesus fast enough. Jesus had started a fire and grilled up fish, and he asked them to bring him the fish they caught at his command.

Jesus met their physical need by serving breakfast to them that morning, and he met their sorrowful souls with his physical presence. He took care of them in that moment, and he hasn't stopped caring for them or for us since.

In Nahum 1:7 we read, "The LORD is good, a refuge in times of trouble. He cares for those who trust in him."

We are free to cast our cares on him because of his great care for us.

He has demonstrated his unbreakable, unbendable, unwavering care for us time and time again. His care for you and me took him to the cross, where he experienced unimaginable pain and ultimately death so that you and I don't have to die the death our sinful nature demands.

We are free to fully trust him and to cast all our cares off and away from us and onto Christ.

His love and care for us is so grand. The Bible tells us that it was "while we were still sinners [that] Christ died for us."[2] And the author of Hebrews wrote that "for the joy set before him [Jesus] endured the cross."[3]

Friend, this joy Hebrews is talking about is what Jesus knew when he willingly went to the cross to die so that you might be free to go to him with all that you are and with all your heart, believing and trusting that he is for you and he is Lord.

As if this isn't enough to nourish our souls and strengthen our trust and love for our Savior Jesus, his care for us is also designed to extend in and through us. Receiving his care equips us to care for others the way he has cared for us.

Peter had no doubt the man on the shore in John's gospel was Jesus because this wasn't the first time Jesus had called out to Peter and commanded him to lower his nets once more, resulting in a massive catch.

Luke pens an account in his gospel, in chapter five, of a moment Jesus showed up in Peter's life roughly three years earlier.

Luke tells us Jesus stepped into Peter's boat and asked him to push off just beyond the shore, probably so that his voice would be magnified to the crowd waiting on the shore, eager for his teaching. Peter did what Jesus said, and when Jesus was done teaching, he told Peter to cast his nets into the waters.

Peter wasted no time in informing Jesus that casting the nets at this time was pointless because he had already spent the entire night at sea, casting his nets over and over again with no result.

How many times do we feel like praying is pointless because we're tired of saying the same things to Jesus and not seeing the results we expect or want? But what if Jesus has more for us in the action of casting our cares on him than we think he does?

Peter said that, because Jesus commanded it, he'd throw out his nets once more. You know how the story goes. The nets caught so many fish that they began to tear, and as Peter and others worked to haul the nets full of fish into their fishing boats, the boats were so weighed down by the fish, they began to sink.

It was then that Peter called Jesus Lord and repented.

Jesus' response? "Don't be afraid; from now on you will fish for people." No longer would Peter be a fisherman; he would be a fisher of men. He had a new calling and a new purpose because of his encounter with Jesus.

In his kindness, Jesus willingly shows up when and where we need him the most. And he reminds us of who we are and of the calling and purpose he has determined for us. We are never too far beyond his reach of mercy, love, and grace; he still invites us back to who he made us to be. Continually. Every day he whispers to you and me, "*Come to me. Cast all your cares upon me. I care deeply for you.*"

And as we see as the story continues to unfold

in John's gospel, there's profound purpose in casting our cares on the Lord and, in exchange, receiving the care he lavishes upon us. Purpose that goes beyond ourselves. Purpose that extends the care of Jesus to the lost, broken, wayward individuals around us.

After breakfast, there by the side of the sea, Jesus restored Peter, who was broken up about the three times he denied knowing Jesus on the night before his crucifixion.

Sometimes we're hesitant to go to Jesus in all things because we feel shame. Shame keeps us from going to Jesus because it causes us to feel bad about ourselves and to isolate ourselves from him and possibly even from others around us.

Before the crucifixion, Peter boldly declared that he would never deny Christ, yet, that's exactly what he did—not once, not two times, but three times—on the night Jesus was arrested and tortured.

Peter was ashamed.

But Jesus reminded Peter to cast his cares upon him. He did so by asking Peter three times if Peter loved him. Three times, the same number of times Peter had denied Christ. With each response to the Lord's questions, Peter was given space to tell the

Lord his love for him. Thus, Peter's relationship to Christ was restored and his shame removed.

Jesus will do the same for you and me every time. Shame has no power over us when Jesus is with us. We don't have to isolate ourselves and hide from him. His invitation to go to him in all things includes when we feel shame. He will receive us with open arms and restore our relationship with him so that nothing comes between him and us.

Jesus didn't stop with merely restoring Peter's relationship to him. He continued with a charge to extend that reach of care to others. With each declaration from Peter, Jesus commanded Peter to extend his care to his flock. In other words, he told Peter to care for others in their time of need.

You and I are built to care for others. This was part of God's design from the start of creation. Our care for those around us, however, is impaired when we hold back from giving our cares to the only one who can free us up from being burdened by them.

When my youngest boy was five and I'd tell him to sit still, he'd say to me, "Mom, I'm not built that way." He was right. He was five, and five-year-old boys are not built to sit still. They come with so much built-in energy and so many wiggles. Being still is not a concept he could grasp. Yet, in his wisdom, he said it was something he just wasn't built for in that season. And he wasn't wrong.

Much of what we experience in this life, we just aren't built for. Carrying burdens, lugging around baggage from the past, schlepping through difficult seasons rife with suffering and pain. We were not built for such things.

We were designed to be in community with one another and to extend the mercy and care of Christ to the world. And we do this best when we're freed up from our burdens and filled up with the love and care of Christ. When we empty ourselves before him, his peace and courage fill us up, enabling us to extend his reach of care to the world around us.

When we cast our concerns with gusto, like my sons have taught me to do by their fishing skills, we free ourselves up to receive what Christ has for us and to ultimately flourish as he designed us to do. And in doing so, we receive the comfort and care of Christ and the courage and ability to comfort and care for those we encounter throughout our lives.

Paul understood this and reminded the Corinthians of this very truth.

"Praise be to the God and Father of our Lord Jesus Christ, the Father of compassion and the God of all comfort, who comforts us in all our troubles, so that we can comfort those in any trouble with the comfort we ourselves receive from God."[4]

Dear reader, what cares are weighing you down today? What concerns are keeping you up at night? What troubles are you facing? Take a few moments right now to pull back your arm and cast them to Jesus. Release your grip on things that weigh you down and, palms open, receive the care and comfort Jesus has for you today.

Finally, extend the care and comfort of Jesus Christ as you go about your day. The world is hurting. Christ is the only balm who can heal.

May his name be known as good and loving in all the world.

A wonderful exchange takes place when we truly cast our cares upon the Lord Jesus. In exchange for our burdens, worries, and cares, in their place, Jesus fills us with more of himself, more of his mercy, grace, joy, contentment, courage, and peace. Jesus fills us up with these things and more and then commands us to cast our net out in care of others.

As we cast our cares upon Jesus, he fills up their space with his presence and enables us to extend care to those in need around us.

Surrendering to the only one who can relieve us of what we were never meant to bear is the only way to a life of freedom and flourishing, the only way to become who we were made to be, so we can do the things we were made for.

Jesus invites us to cast our cares onto him.

CHAPTER 7

Invited to Today

I once heard the testimony of a ninety-five-year-old woman. Ninety-five years of life is a long time. Ninety-five years of life! Her pockets must have been deep with both highs and lows of life. She likely had an ocean of experiences she could have drawn from to share with us, but she didn't tell stories from her lived experiences as one would expect. She didn't share her life's story. Instead, she simply said that Jesus walked with her, his hand in hers, throughout all her life. She simply shared that walking with him is the greatest thing we can do with our lives.

The thing about walking with Christ is that we step when he steps. We stop when he stops. We run when he runs. At least, that's the idea. Walking with Christ almost never looks like a perfect two-step, and this is just one of the countless reasons his grace is so amazing.

He leads. We follow.

It's nearly impossible for us to constantly walk in step with Jesus. We cannot see tomorrow, let alone five seconds from now. We are limited in space and time and have extremely limited understanding of all that goes on around us on any given day. Sometimes we run way ahead of where Jesus is, such as when we feel confident that we know the way forward and don't really see the need to consult with him. And sometimes we slow to a stop in fear or rebellion as he moves forward.

Some of us live with regret regarding the past while others of us tend to worry and feel anxious or afraid of what may come tomorrow.

But when we are in these spaces, Jesus' tender heart swells with compassion, and he gently whispers an invitation to move in sync with him again. And he does so again the next day, when we get off course. And then again when it happens ten minutes after the last time.

Jesus is steady on the ready.

He modeled this so well for us when he lived his earthly life. He was born a baby, which meant he had to go through all the developmental stages a baby in the womb goes through before he even took his first breath. The King of the universe entered time and space and waited patiently upon God as he orchestrated all of life's events from the womb to the tomb. Jesus' entire life was lived according to the timeline of the Father's will and design. He didn't rush ahead or stop by his own accord. He didn't get stuck in the past or rush to the future.

As the Father willed and commanded, Jesus obeyed and followed. Even to death on a cross.

He walked perfectly in step with God's design for his human experience, which is exactly why he's the most understanding person we can go to when we're tempted to run ahead of or stay back from where he is as he leads.

When he was in the garden praying on the night before his crucifixion, he was not shy about wanting to not go through the torture he knew was coming. And yet, he said he would obey and carry out the will of the Father. This was Jesus keeping in step with God, even when it was difficult.

We will never experience the magnitude of suffering that Christ did upon the cross. The physical suffering was so bad, it's difficult to put into words. Scripture says that Jesus was beaten beyond recognition. But his suffering didn't stop there. The greatest suffering of all was the moment God forsook his Son, Jesus, on the cross. For the first time ever, Jesus was separated from the Father. There was a moment there, as he took his final breath, when God had forsaken him and he suffered alone.

Why would he do this? Because he knew that although it was painful, taking on our sin and the wrath of God in our place meant we might never be separated from God. We will never know what it's like to not be in God's presence, on this earth and in heaven to come, because Jesus endured momentary separation and suffering for our sins on the cross.

He gets it. He lived it. He understands what it feels like to be out of step with God. He is full of grace and understanding every time we're tempted to wander away from where he is or not keep the pace as he leads. He will never tire of beckoning us back to him, no matter how many steps ahead or behind we may find ourselves. He's the living God who desires to walk with us every minute of every day.

The J Men and I participated in a 5K race not too long ago. I trained five days a week leading up to the race and had worked my way up to running a mile without needing to walk so I was hopeful I could at least run the first mile with them. When the racing gun went off, the boys left me in the dust. They took off and my legs were moving, but my pace was only a hair faster than a mall walk. I ended up jogging a little bit and then walking for a short time before jogging some more.

I walked the last half mile, trying to talk myself into running the final stretch across the finish line even though all I wanted to do at that point was lie down on the asphalt and take a nap. I was wiped from my jog/walk excursion. I felt someone gaining on me so I turned my weary head over my right shoulder and saw a woman about twenty years older than me, walking faster than I was at that moment.

As she passed me, she said, "I can't believe I used to run these things. I just walk now, and that's enough for me." Excuse me, come again? Here I had tired myself out from my jog/walk routine and a woman with twenty years on me passed me by and crossed the finish line before me with her steady walk.

I felt like the fool watching wisdom walk on by.

She knew her pace, and she stuck with it for the duration of the race.

There's so much wisdom to be had in knowing our pace, running our race, and walking with steadfast purpose reflective of who God designed us to be and how he equipped us to live.

Joseph is one biblical example that comes to mind when I think about running ahead of God's design, getting off course, and then experiencing grace by finding our way again after many years and many trials.

At a young age, Joseph believed he'd be somebody powerful one day. His life would be important and others would take note. Especially his older brothers. His father already favored him due to his wild love for Joseph's mom, who was openly loved more than the mothers of Jospeh's older brothers. Joseph's family was plagued by jealousy.

So when Joseph told his older brothers that one day he'd be important and they would bow to him in reverence, they didn't take it too well. They plotted to kill him. It was the oldest brother, Reuben, who talked them out of killing him immediately. Then another brother, Judah, came up with the plan of selling him to slave traders headed for Egypt. So that's what they did. Then they covered up it all up. Their father Jacob believed Joseph was dead, and the brothers kept the truth a secret for many years.

It's such a relatable story, because how many of us know in our guts we were made for more than we experience on any given day? How many of us have dreams and hopes for the future that drive us and give us purpose? How many of us have intuitions about who we could be and what God made us for? We want to run ahead and arrive at our full potential, but no matter how hard we try, we fall short every time.

Or the opposite is true. We know our potential, we sense the calling God has on our life, but we're afraid of it. So, we ignore it, hush the encouraging voice, and try to busy ourselves with other responsibilities rather than face our fear.

Regardless of your pace on the race today, Jesus invites you to walk in step with him. He gave us his example of how to be in the present and not worry about tomorrow or fret about the past.

One of the most difficult tasks of my life has been learning to surrender to the moment. I like sprinting ahead. It energizes me and gives me a momentary high I enjoy. And other times I am quick to put the brakes on when I feel Christ's leading is too scary or too much for me to handle in the moment.

Both scenarios lead to anxiety and fear, and we all know how those two clowns lead to a pit that's difficult to climb out of. Nobody has time for that.

Jesus is the better way who continually invites us to remain present with the him, the Prince of Peace.

It may not be easy to remain in step with Jesus, but it certainly is the better pace to keep. Better for our souls, our families, our passions and desires, and our overall well-being.

Aside from the two years I lived in Massachusetts for grad school, I never imagined I would live outside southern California. I was born and raised near the beach in Orange County, and why would I ever want to move away from such a lovely place? I loved living in California. It's a beautiful place and, in many ways, will always be my home. But something strange and unexpected happened in the late spring of 2021 (five or so months from the day I felt pressed to read 1 Peter in Sedona). I began to wonder how life might be different, more fulfilling, more adventurous, and, let's be real, less expensive, if we moved out of California.

It would be eighteen months from the initial thought of moving out of California until it happened. Eighteen months of seeking God's will about a move out of California, exploring options of when and where to move, and trusting that the stirring I felt deep down in my guts was truly God and not the fish tacos I'd had for lunch. I had to know for certain such a move was really from him before a move that big could ever happen.

The more I sought what to do from the Lord, the more confident I grew that a move outside of my home state was inevitable.

But the waiting period was rough. Slowly and over time, I no longer felt at home in California, a feeling foreign to me up to this point in my life. All the while, we didn't know where we would end up or when. From the moment I felt released from California and began the hunt for a new state to call home, I wanted it all to happen fast. My mind was made up; we were moving, so why put off the inevitable? Eighteen months went by before we felt clear we were headed to the Lone Star State.

Living in the present during this season of waiting was not easy. I kept a journal and would often write about how difficult it was to feel the pull to leave my home state, while simultaneously not knowing where we'd end up or a single logistic about when, where, or how the move would unfold. The journal helped me process all the unknowns and reminded me to daily anchor myself in the truth that Jesus had all the details down. He had all the answers. I didn't need to know all the things; I needed only to know him and to trust him enough to follow his lead one day at a time.

I remember doing a Kelly Minter study called *Finding God Faithful: A Study on the Life of Joseph*,[1] during this season of waiting. Yes, the same Joseph who got ahead of himself and whose brothers sold him to slave traders on their way to Egypt. There's a short verse in his story found in Genesis that's too easy to miss: "When two full years had passed…"[2]

Joseph was in jail and forgotten about for two years. Two years!

The guy who so confidently knew God had

designed him for greatness was forgotten about in prison for two whole, long years.

We read that tiny verse and are on to the next one in two seconds flat. Two seconds to capture two years. We can't possibly understand all Joseph experienced, the hopeful highs and the depressing despair, in a two-second thought.

I get impatient after two days, sometimes two hours, and, most often, let's be honest, after two minutes.

I wonder what Joseph's prayers were like during this season. He had been through so much before this point—the dream, the brothers, slavery, and now jail. His life was a roller coaster. In jail, he met a fellow prisoner, and when that guy was released before Joseph, Joseph asked to remember him, speak to the Pharoah on his behalf, and have him released. Upon his release, the dude forgot about Joseph nor did he mention Joseph to Pharoah.

But the Lord God never forgets his people. Dear reader, he hasn't forgotten you either.

The hope Joseph must have felt in the days following his fellow prisoner's release! Surely, today, would be the day of his release. If not today, then tomorrow. Freedom must surely have been around the corner. Yet, for over two years, he remained bound, confined to a jail. And it was a jail he did not deserve to be confined to. It had been a false accusation that landed him in jail.

I wonder if he pleaded with God to reaffirm his promises to him. I wonder if he questioned what he had at one time felt so confident in. I wonder if he doubted the dreams he had as a young boy and felt regret for words exchanged with his siblings.

I wonder if he lived with regret for the past and full of anxiety for his future.

The Bible is full of story after story of God delivering a promise followed by a season of waiting, often long periods of time, and finally fulfillment of the promise. Typically, the fulfillment part looks nothing like we expected it would. And often, the fulfillment of promise isn't actualized until the one who received the promise has passed. And yet, the charge to us all to remain in step with Jesus and to keep the faith day in and day out remains, with no guarantee we'll see promises fulfilled in our lifetime.

The waiting creates space for learning to trust the only one who holds our life in his hands.

A life walked with Jesus is a long game of learning to trust him, step by step.

Abraham provides for us a great example. God promised Abraham he would be the father of many nations and many people would be blessed through him. Twenty-five years passed from the time God made his promise to Abraham until the birth of Isaac.

And during the long twenty-five-year period, Abraham made a lot of mistakes. At times, he took matters into his own hands in failed attempts to speed up God's plan. But we know God used this time to show Abraham how his way was better and that Abraham could trust him. During the waiting, Abraham grew in his faith and trust in God.

By the time of the gut-wrenching story of Abraham and Isaac upon the mountain for the sacrifice commanded by God, we see full abandonment and an Abraham willing to obey every detail of God's command with complete trust in the Lord.

It takes time to grow in faith and trust and that's okay. Jesus is incredibly understanding and patient.

The sweetness found in a surrendered life that walks in step with Christ daily is deeply tethered to trust in a God who is full of goodness and wisdom.

When we get a taste of just how good he really is, we're likely to find joy in full abandonment of self and grow in reliance upon him.

Dane Ortlund puts it this way: "Glad abandon is our only sanity."[3]

We find our joy and all that we need today, in this very moment, not when we're looking for it, but when we're looking at Jesus. Yielding to his way today leads us straight to him every time. And in him, we find our joy, peace, contentment, and gratitude. Apart from him, glimpses of these things may appear from time to time in spurts here and there, but they won't last. Keeping our eyes fixed on Jesus and our hearts attuned to him and his ways produces in us change with eternal impact. We will be the kind of people who get to the end of our lives and whose testimony is "Jesus walked with me."

Learning the sweetness of surrender is a lifelong process.

And that's a good thing. Too often we opt for the air fryer approach to life because it's quick and delivers what we want when we want it. But ultimately, what we need is a slow cooker. We need time to marinate, simmer, and slowly come to readiness.

When my youngest son was four, he asked me to cook pasta for him. I put the pot of water on the stove and cranked up the heat. As soon as the water began to boil, I dumped in the pasta. He was apparently really hungry, because before the pasta was fully cooked, he began to beg me to wrap up the cooking process and serve him immediately. I assured him the pasta was not yet cooked and he proceeded to tell me how much he didn't care. He was ready to eat and it was "done enough."

Most of my days, I am tempted to get ahead and outpace the one who ordains my steps. I'm tempted to accept good, rather than wait for great. Too often I settle for "done enough." The promises of God are equally important as the process of trusting the promise on the steady road towards the finish line. The promise isn't more important than the process. They are equal parts with Jesus by your side.

Jesus has so much more for us than living trapped by yesterday's regrets or so far ahead in our minds that we're anxious for tomorrow. His mercy and grace are enough for today.

Jesus invites us to live fully present today, trusting that he has tomorrow in his hands.

CHAPTER 8

Invited to Give It Up

When my oldest son was just three years old, he was into the Curious George cartoons. He loved that little monkey and the mischief he found himself in with each new episode. One day, I took my son with me to meet up with coworkers of mine for lunch, one of whom was named George. It never occurred to me that my son would think he was actually going to lunch with Curious George. However, my mistake quickly became apparent as we walked towards George and my son looked around and beyond George for the individual he was expecting to meet for lunch that day.

The oldest J Man was very confused that I greeted my coworker George with "Hi, George" when the Curious George he was expecting was nowhere in sight.

In any season of life, we can feel confident things will go this way or that way, when in reality, we are limited by our line of sight, perception, and understanding. Only God sees all, knows all, and understands all rightly.

My son was so disappointed when he realized George was just an average dude I worked with and not an ornery little monkey. A large order of fries for lunch helped ease the sting of his disappointment in the moment, but was he very bummed coworker George was not the same as monkey George.

My son was very impressionable at that age. His understanding of the situation was so far from reality because of his limits as a child. And as his mom, I wasn't mad at him, and I certainly didn't cause him to feel like an idiot because he actually believed he was meeting Curious George for lunch. It was the exact opposite, actually. My momma heart was softened and tender towards him.

God has proven himself the same when it comes to our disappointments over the unmet expectations in our lives. He's not angry or mad when we have specific expectations regarding how we desire our lives to go. Rather, I believe he's tender towards us and patient with us. For most of us, our expectations are good, but his plan is better, and sometimes it's difficult for us to see and understand that in the moment.

Things may not pan out the way we hoped they would from our limited perspective, but God's way is fuller, richer, and more purposeful than the way we might imagine for ourselves. And it's often later when we have the hindsight to see and know this to be true.

When I went to seminary and studied cross-cultural evangelism, it was for the purpose of graduating and serving somewhere in Africa as a missionary. I spent two years studying the Christian faith around the globe. I longed to learn how to share the gospel message so that it spoke to a person's heart in a transformative way, and I hoped to ultimately change communities for generations to come.

During my time as a student, I was given a large piece of paper with the outline of every country in the world on it as a midterm exam. The objective of the test was to fill in the name of every country on the blank map. I loved studying for and taking that exam. In fact, it was the only exam I've ever loved. Just the mere thought of any other exam, such as Greek 101, to name just one, and I break out in hives. But not when it comes to the world. I geek out on cultures and countries other than my own, especially when it comes to the idea of sharing the good news of the gospel in them.

My goal was to graduate, move abroad, love on people who were culturally very different than me, and simply share a message of God's love for them.

And that's not at all how my story went. It's been two decades since graduation, and I have never lived abroad, and I have never worked as a missionary.

And yet, the longing in my heart to immerse myself in a culture other than my own and the desire to share the love of God with others has never gone away. The desire remains, but how that desire is lived out is very different than what I imagined. It's taken some time and an ocean of questions directed at God, but I can now look back on the past twenty years and see the fruit of my unmet expectations.

There are several examples we could turn to in Scripture to highlight this truth, but Daniel comes to mind now as someone who faced a world of disappointment and was forced to navigate a life of unmet expectations. Ultimately, he resolved to stick with God in the face of disappointment and unmet expectations, but it came with a high cost.

Before Daniel made friends with lions in a den, he was a young man living in his homeland of Judah. Daniel had friends and family and a future ahead of him. Like all young people do, he surely had dreams and hopes for his future. He likely desired a family and the opportunity to pursue his passions. He may have daydreamed about coming home from a hard day's work to embrace his wife and roughhouse with his kids before dinner.

The first chapter of his namesake book in the Bible tells us a very different story. His hopes and expectations for how his life might go took a sharp left one day, and his life was never the same. His roots in Judah were ripped up and turned on their heads. His plans and hopes for his future were taken from him in an instant.

Daniel found himself in survival mode in an absolute nightmare situation. Along with his entire community, Daniel had been captured by Babylon. Babylon was the cruelest, most oppressive society in Daniel's day. When the Babylonians came through, they stripped the land of all it had to offer, taking for themselves what they pleased.

Daniel, a devout citizen of Judah and follower of the Lord's way, quite possibly questioned how any of this could have been God's plan. Daniel and many others had no choice but to give up their old way of living and adapt to their new life as captives of Babylon.

Their landscape changed. The food they were accustomed to eating was now different. Their way of living was no longer an option. They were expected to live the Babylonian way and were no longer free to pursue their dreams and desires. They were captives.

I'm going to venture to say not one reader of this little book is a captive of a foreign nation. But I would also venture to say every one of us has had hopes and dreams and expectations ripped out from under our feet. As you read the words on this page, it's likely there are many areas of life that just aren't going like you wish they would. Though not a captive of a foreign land, you may feel trapped within circumstances you'd rather not be in, in this season. And you're not alone. I'm right there with you floating through the sea of letdown.

Perhaps your marriage isn't where you'd like it to be. Maybe your kids aren't where you'd like them be. It could be that your career is a bit stagnant, and you're disappointed you aren't further along on your career path. You're not as healthy as you had hoped you'd be by this time in your life. You feel behind your peers. You feel let down. You're disappointed.

When we come face-to-face with letdown, disappointment, and our unmet expectations, we also find ourselves at a fork in the road with a choice to make. We can either choose to remain with the Lord and trust him in the midst of our sorrow and grief over the loss of how we thought life would pan out, or we can walk away.

The amazing thing is, even if we choose to walk away from him out of our despair, we can never venture so far that he will lose sight of us. There is no place our feet could ever wander that is beyond his reach. Nor is there a distance our hearts may travel apart from him that he is unable to bridge in order to bring us back to himself.

Jesus is incredibly patient and kind. He's not afraid of or annoyed by our wandering tendencies. He understands how bent toward sin our hearts are and how strongly the pull to live independently of him grips us. But thank him, his grip on us is stronger.

The amazing thing about grace is that it can find us no matter where we are. It moves in and through the muck and frustration we face and has the ability to reach the deepest well of our souls, wrap itself around us, and hold on tight.

All the while, it whispers in a gentle and tender voice to the place in our heart where we need to hear it most. I imagine the whisper of grace saying, "Give it up."

Give *it* up, whatever *it* is for you. Give it to the Lord and seize the opportunity to receive all things Jesus has designed and prepared instead.

Give up worry and receive rest.

Give up anxiety and receive peace.

Give up perfectionism and receive acceptance.

Give up people-pleasing and receive freedom. Give up trying to do all and be all and receive contentment.

Jesus invites us to give it all up—and not just for the sake of freeing our lives of the things that so easily weigh us down, but so that our hands and our arms are free to receive the gift of knowing him and all the things that come with a relationship with him. Gifts like rest, peace, joy, and contentment—the things this world tells us we can earn and achieve on our own with hard work and a little bit of elbow grease. But the truth is, only in Jesus is our every longing and every need satisfied.

Jesus said he came to give life and to give it abundantly.[1]

What an opportunity we have to live a different story by giving it all up to Jesus and, with outstretched arms, receiving all we need and more from him directly, personally, and lovingly! It might not be the story we expected would be ours, but it will certainly be a story that surpasses our expectations in ways we could never have imagined.

So, no, I didn't move to Africa and serve a community as a resident missionary like I had hoped and expected upon graduating with a missiology degree. But the Lord brought me an African man to be my husband and our home is an expression of cross-cultural ministry every day. Life looks very different than I thought it would, and yet, I'm more reliant on Jesus and inclined to consult with him on all things. I'm not sure I would be as dependent on him if I were in Africa today.

The Lord knows the desires of our hearts. He

created us to have desires and hopes for our lives. Our perspectives on how these dreams may pan out is almost always skewed by the upside-down, cracked world we live in, but he knows that. And he tenderly and compassionately comes alongside us and whispers, *"Give it up to me, and in return, I will give you more than you could ever imagine."*

We give it up to create space to be filled up with the things of Jesus. This is the sweet spot of a life surrendered to Christ.

The life Daniel had quite possibly imagined would be his one day never happened. He lived out his days a captive in a foreign land. And yet, it was in an unexpected place that he grew an unwavering dependence upon God. His faith grew strong. His resolve unshakable. His courage undeterred. His confidence in the Lord unstoppable.

He had no choice but to give up his hopes in order to receive the only hope that sustains.

What if Jesus is inviting us to give up whatever the thing is that we think we need to white-knuckle hold on to, because the gifts he has for us are more fulfilling and purposeful than we could ever hope or imagine on our own?

Jesus invites us to give it up and receive more than we could ever expect or imagine from him.

CHAPTER 9

Invited to Peace

Growing up, we used to sing hymns on repeat every Sunday morning. The worship leader, who was often my dad at our tiny country Baptist church, would tell us what page to turn to in our hymnal, and all together, as a small congregation made up of all ages and stages, we would sing these words over and over:

> All to Jesus I surrender,
> All to Him I freely give;
> I will ever love and trust Him,
> In His presence daily live.
> I surrender all, I surrender all;
> All to Thee, my blessed Savior,
> I surrender all.

All to Jesus I surrender,
Make me, Savior, wholly Thine;
Let me feel Thy Holy Spirit,
Truly know that Thou art mine.
I surrender all, I surrender all;
All to Thee, my blessed Savior,
I surrender all.
All to Jesus I surrender,
Lord, I give myself to Thee;
Fill me with Thy love and power,
Let Thy blessing fall on me.
I surrender all, I surrender all;
All to Thee, my blessed Savior,
I surrender all.[1]

Of course, my adolescent self could have never imagined just how wonderful these lyrics are and the path toward freedom they'd illuminate as I got older.

In fact, the older I get, the less I care about obtaining outward, flashy things. I imagine the same is true for you. I'm not impressed by high-end cars and am more than content to drive a mediocre one that gets me from A to B and has air conditioning. AC is a must in Florida. I do not care at all what brand of jeans I wear—or that you wear, for that matter. (Although I have been told to steer clear of any jeans I can find at Costco. Apparently, you're really old if you buy your clothes at the same store where you buy your cereal). I will yawn out of boredom listening to someone share their accolades. These things simply matter less and less the older we grow.

But do you know what I long for and strongly desire in my life? (I have a funny feeling it may be the longing of your heart too.) I long for what no amount of money or good jeans could buy.

I long for peace.

I need it like I need the air in my lungs.

I'm increasingly drawn to stories of people who live a life of peace. Notice I did not say a life that looks put together on Instagram or seems to have its ducks in a row. Actually, it's often quite the opposite. I'm magnetic-beam attracted to stories of folks who experience peace with absolute, colossal chaos swirling around them.

The individual with the hard story wearing a sweater of peace in the midst of the hard is the one I'm most impressed by and drawn to. I want peace to be a marker on my life too.

Living from within a puddle of peace has a

ripple effect on every other area of our life as well as on those around us. The private matters of the heart, and knowing and experiencing peace within my soul, are of greater value than anything exterior.

Peace is what flows from a life reconciled and surrendered to Christ. It's a one-time deal. It's not a payment plan you have to earn little by little with good looks or behavior. You can't earn peace. It's a free gift that can only be received in full from the Prince of Peace himself. The peace we receive in this deal cannot be shaken or taken.

There's another old hymn that talks about peace like a river, peace that flows from knowing Christ and trusting him no matter what. The song was written out of gut-wrenching circumstances a husband and a father faced. A fire ruined him financially; his wife and children were killed at sea. This guy was a modern-day Job. Tragedy after tragedy struck him. And somewhere along the way, the peace only Jesus can deposit into a soul invaded and overwhelmed his heart. In the overflow of that peace, "It Is Well with My Soul" was written.

The lyrics of this old song continue to remind us today of Christ's unwavering presence in the midst of chaos and loss and of his gift of perfect peace that he so willingly and freely gives me and you.

Peace is a sweet gift he gives to let us know he's got our back as we face trials and struggles of all kinds. Peace is his love language to us. Peace is the gateway to a life lived in freedom and flourishing, as we believe and cling to the truth that Jesus is good and can be trusted.

When we learned the Pilot's new job was in Florida after less than a year of living in Texas, I had every reason to enter full-on freak-out mode. We had lived in the Lone Star State less than a year when we realized a move to Florida was inevitable.

When we bought our house in Texas, I thought we would be there for some time. Once the boxes were unpacked, I wasted no time turning the house into a home we could really settle into. I spent hours working to put my own personal touch throughout the home. I painted walls. I added character to the walls with board and batten. I gave the pantry a much-needed facelift by adding functional cabinetry topped with a gorgeous

American Oak–stained shelf. I worked hard at making our new Texas house truly a home for our family.

And after only eleven months, we learned our little family of four was Florida-bound.

If you read my first book, *That's For Sure*, you know I am not a fan of creatures with feathers and fur, such as creepy birds and vile cats. For the record, since our move to the Sunshine State, I need to add creatures with scales to the list of those that completely freak me out. Florida is crawling with lizards and alligators. And frogs too.

Please send help. I am unwell.

God knows I come near stroke status when in close proximity to such critters and creatures of the wild. These beasts should remain in the wild. When they creep into the spaces of the humans, namely this human, I come undone. In fact, those were the exact words that came out of my mouth not too long ago when my youngest son found a toad near our kitchen pantry. A *toad*! Living in Florida is for sure going to age me quickly. There is nothing peaceful about a toad *in my house*!

And yet, I have experienced an increased dose of peace since surrendering to the reality that Florida is where God has my family in this season.

Despite the alligators, lizards, pterodactyl-sized birds, and eight million species of bugs who apparently love Florida, I have peace.

I have peace because I've surrendered to God's plan for my life. I have peace because I'm not holding too tightly to what I thought my life would like look according to my plans. I have peace because I'm holding loosely to the things I have and the place where I am today, so that my hands are free to grasp on to what Jesus has for me and for my family in this season. In a posture of surrender, my arms and hands are in the air, palms up, in praise and ready to receive what Jesus has planned and designed for me and my family.

I'm using a silly example of living in peace while surrounded by Jurassic Park–type wildlife to make the point that peace is possible and available to all of us. But I know all too well, and so do you, that in this life we have and will likely continue to experience really unsettling times. And is the peace of Christ available and active during those trying times too? Absolutely.

But in this very moment, as you're reading the words on this page, let me ask you, friend, where do you need the peace of Christ to invade and overwhelm you? What unfortunate and unwanted circumstance is swirling around you with the threat of overtaking you? What dream or expectation—a person or a plan for your life—are you gripping too tightly, preventing you from openhandedly receiving the gift of peace and so much more that Jesus longs to give you?

I have a friend with the most calming, peaceful voice. Do you know these people? You know, the person you call when you're frazzled and the moment they answer the phone, their calming voice and wise words soothe your soul?

For me, this is my friend Dalia. Dalia and I worked together for a season, and it took no time at all for her voice to become a trusted one in my life and for her to become a cherished friend. More than twenty-five years have passed since we were coworkers, and yet she continues to be a trusted voice in my life today. She's steady and calm. She has a peace about her that is so clearly deeply webbed into the walls of her soul.

When she speaks, peace flows from her.

I like to call it *peace out*. See what I did there?

When Jesus gives us the gift of his peace, it's

never meant to remain solely with us.

The kind of peace he gives is intended to bubble up and overflow out into every area of our lives, so that it permeates every aspect of our lives and the runoff touches those around us. When I'm living in the peace Jesus designed for me, my marriage, my kids, and my community reap the benefits.

Peace begets peace.

So how do we let go of the angst and grasp the peace of Christ? Like the song lyrics that this chapter began with, *all to Him we freely give*. This part is worth repeating: *all*.

We don't just give our hearts to Jesus the moment we declare him Lord and Savior of our lives, and then magically our problems fade away. Jesus doesn't cause the circumstances of this life to disappear. Rather, he steps into the circumstances with us. He walks right beside us.

As it turns out, experiencing his presence with us in the chaos is better than the chaos disappearing altogether.

Every day, we must loosen our grip on the things we think are best for our lives and begin to hold tightly to the things he has designed for us. Every minute of every day, we must choose to go about our day cognizant that our life is not our own, but belongs to him. And because we belong to him, we can exhale and rest, trusting he has a far better path paved for us than could ever be possible apart from him.

This act of surrender isn't a one and done. It's a daily decision we make, and often it's an hour by hour, minute by minute choice to walk with Christ and to openhandedly receive all he designed and desires to give us.

Staying the course and walking with Jesus, when everything around you screams, "Abort, abort, turn this ship around," is incredibly hard *and* so worth the peace that will inevitably flow from a life in step with the one who cares more deeply for you than you'll ever comprehend.

Learning to remain and stand still with Jesus is not easy, but it is simple. Over time, choosing to keep open dialogue with Jesus about the thing that is most difficult to surrender creates space for Jesus to show us he's trustworthy.

Walk steady—keep the course and fix your eyes on the goal regardless of obstacles.

Surrender is never fully achieved in this life. We can't check it off a list and say, "I surrender and now I'm good for life." Instead, it's a daily choice we must make to remain tethered to Jesus and actively trust him today, for today. And when tomorrow comes with all that may come with it, we choose to remain with Jesus, we choose to yield to his design, and we choose to rest in his presence. His peace is ours for the keeping. And it will flow like a river, winding and bending throughout all corners of our world, and the runoff will flow into the lives of the people we care most about.

Peace out, friend.

Jesus invites us to receive the gift of his peace regardless of life's circumstances.

CHAPTER 10

Invited to Run Home

In the summer months of 2005, I spent six weeks in Moldova. Moldova is a beautiful country with even more beautiful people. My trip had a twofold purpose. As part of my graduate program at Gordon-Conwell Theological Seminary, I was required to spend six weeks abroad to gain hands-on experience as a missionary. Most of my class went to Zimbabwe. But I was also working at a church as a youth leader that summer, and their teens regularly took a short-term trip to a church partner they had in Moldova. I decided to complete my six weeks in Moldova so that I could also be available to lead the teens.

During my stay, I met a group of missionaries serving with Youth with a Mission (YWAM). As a group, they had spent three months on a ship learning what it meant to share Christ cross-culturally. By the time I met the group of twentysomethings, they were completing their mission with a land assignment in Moldova.

Iain, who was from England, and I hit it off right away. Iain was a trained dentist and very kind. He first heard the gospel from Billy Graham at a festival when he was just a young boy. He grew to love the idea of sharing about Christ in a cross-cultural setting.

On one particular evening, Iain and I grabbed some dinner in downtown. Both of us had been warned not to be out too late; as a tall Englishman and an American lady, as we were sure to draw unwanted attention.

But we were so engrossed in conversation, we didn't realize the time. It was late. It was dark. We knew we needed to get on our way.

We left the restaurant and began walking down a city block toward an area we believed would likely have taxis waiting to give us a lift back to the respective places we were staying. (If you read my first book, *That's For Sure*, you'll know I was staying with Tatyana, the sweetest woman, who had a bird who swooped down and ate my breakfast toast before I could get a bite in.)

Iain and I were not far from the restaurant when two men approached and stopped us. They spoke Romanian in a harsh tone, and neither Iain or I could understand a word they were saying but we got the impression they wanted to see our passports. We didn't have our passports on us, and even if we did, we were not about to give these guys our identification. They claimed to be police, but again, they were in plain clothes. How were we to know if they could be trusted?

They raised their voices and demanded our passports. I wasn't sure how we were going to get out of this one.

When it was clear they couldn't understand what we were saying in response to their demands, Iain came up with the best plan he could think of on the fly. He told me that on his count of three, I was to run away from stranger danger as fast as I could, and we'd both go 'round the corner, where we hoped we'd find taxis waiting.

One...two...three. Run!

And boy did I run. We booked it down to the end of the block, around the corner, and, thank the good Lord, we found a row of taxis waiting to pick folks up. Iain told me to jump in the first car, and he jumped in the one right behind. I told the driver to "go" and he put the petal to the metal. The plainclothes "police officers" turned the corner just as my driver pulled away from the curb.

We ran away from danger and, thankfully, Iain and I made it to where we staying safely.

We find a lot of running language in Scripture. Paul uses running language in his letters to the first churches quite a bit. He talks about running our race and keeping our eyes on the prize, which is eternity with Jesus. We run expectant of the finish line.

But Paul wasn't the only one who referenced running in Scripture.

My favorite running story in the Bible is that of Mary Magdalene. She's not typically someone we remember as a runner, but the Bible tells us she may have run the greatest run of all time. Mary ran away from the grave that could not keep the body of Jesus.[1] The Bible describes Mary as afraid and full of joy as she ran away from the grave.

Later that day, she saw the risen Lord Jesus alive and well. In fact, he called her by name—a moment in Scripture that makes emotion well up in me.[2] Jesus showed up in the midst of what was arguably Mary's most devastating moment: the moment when she was contemplating the empty tomb and fearing thieves had stolen his lifeless body. Her heart must have felt like a brick sinking to the bottom of the ocean.

It had been hard enough to watch the one who had saved her from a life of abuse and trauma die. Jesus had restored her hope in the better way he promised when he described his kingdom come. Then he died. And then to have stumbled upon an empty tomb? Her hope must have been shattered.

And it was in this moment, maybe her lowest ever, that Jesus stood before her, scars in his hands, kindness in his eyes, and said, "*Mary*."[3]

And I imagine Mary was once again afraid and full of joy.

Jesus has a way of giving us joy, even when we're afraid. Just as he called Mary by name, he knows our names and he stands before and beside us, cheering us on as we run this race called life.

And just like Mary did when she heard the news that the grave was empty, I think the invitation stands for us to run away from the things in this life that bring destruction and death and, instead, to run, with joy, toward life. Even when we're afraid.

Mary's hope was restored when she heard Jesus speak her name.

Is there an area in your life where you need hope restored? Does it feel like you're in an impossible situation with no way out? Are you struggling to find joy?

There are times in my life when I feel tempted to move towards the areas of my life I know are dead. Jesus is alive and I've been made alive in him, but I still feel the pull of temptation back towards the grave. It's so easy to feel overwhelmed by life and, without a second thought, to revert back to old patterns of thinking. It's easy for me to take things into my own hands in an attempt to fight or fix. Too easily, I can lose sight of the risen Jesus and look to myself for answers and solutions to my life's problems and challenges.

I wonder if Mary's mind, when she saw the empty tomb and suspected someone stole Jesus' body, raced with ideas about what to do and how to fix the problem she faced. I wonder if she thought those years of following Jesus might have been for naught. I wonder if she thought about returning to her old way of life.

Jesus is too kind to have let that happen to Mary, and he's too kind to leave you where you are today. He's very much alive and well and involved in your life. He continually invites you and me to run away from the grave and out into the world with the good news of his resurrection.

The part about Mary being afraid is not lost on me. I think fear may be the biggest reason we don't do more running away from our old ways and toward the world with good news.

We're afraid and fear paralyzes us.

We want to run our race. We want to share our faith. We want to live a life worthy of our calling.

But we're afraid. Living in fear keeps us safe. Or so we think. Fear keeps us from taking risks and from trying new things. Fear isolates us and silences us.

Running with abandon and without hinderance with the good news of Jesus is risky. What if others don't believe us? What if they give us a hard time and think we're nuts? What if we don't communicate well and our words sound more crazy than true?

When Jesus told Mary to go tell the others that he was alive, he didn't say they would believe her. He didn't tell her she wouldn't face any opposition. He just told her to go and she went.

The same is true for us today. We can't see

what's going to happen five seconds from now. We don't know how those in our workplaces and in our families and the stranger in line at the grocery store may respond to the message. We don't get to know that beforehand. We're simply charged to run and deliver the message. We're the couriers of the good news.

Paul talked a little bit about this when he said, "How beautiful are the feet of those who bring good news!"[4]

The Bible says that "while we were still sinners, Christ died for us."[5]

Before Christ saved us and called his own, we were like the walking dead: breathing, but dead inside. And we were headed for the grave. But in his kindness and mercy, Christ died the death we deserved because of our sin and, in exchange, he clothed us in his righteousness and made us new.

We may be afraid like Mary surely was, but joy will be our story.

Because of Jesus, we get to run away from the grave too.

Like Mary, you and I are invited to run away from the tomb and into the world around us with the news that Jesus lives. Jesus is the better way. He invites us to run into the dark places where hope has no name and speak his name so that hope may be restored for more and more and more and more.

I want my life to be a joyful sprint toward what matters most.

Jesus invites us to leave the old way behind and, instead, run towards life with joy in our hearts.

CHAPTER 11

Invited to Flourish

When my husband, the Pilot, graduated from officer training school at the United States Coast Guard training academy as a pilot for the National Oceanic and Atmospheric Association, my sons and I watched proudly as the graduates performed a ceremony on the front lawn before the graduation itself. Each person had their position. Every one of them had a specific role to carry out and remaining in their place to complete their specific part was key to not only fulfilling their individual role, but to the success of the entire class.

Had any one of the new grads gone rogue and begun to go their own way or do their own thing, chaos would've erupted on the field, and graduates and spectators alike would've been confused.

My sons and I watched proudly as the Pilot and his unit marched in uniform and in perfect formation before us. We were filled with joy and pride as we witnessed the Pilot play his part with purpose and confidence. He knew exactly what he needed to do and he did it well.

I think God smiles and loves watching us, men and women formed in his image, walking the specific path he's designed us to walk upon. When we know who he is and why he made us, we are free to step confidently toward his purposes for our lives. What a beautiful thing!

The opposite is forging our own way, apart from what God has designed for us. The Bible tells us repeatedly that our own path will inevitably lead us to destruction and death.

∽

Jeremiah was a young man when the Lord appeared to him, told him for what purpose he had been made, and gave him his mission. Jeremiah became a prophet during a time when God's people were forging their own path and had forsaken the ways of God.

Jeremiah felt ill-equipped for the call and made

a couple attempts to change God's mind. He was quick to tell God that he was young and not a great speaker. How could he be a prophet whose job was to deliver God's message to the Israelite people?

I'm also quick to offer up excuses to explain why God's got it wrong. Surely, he has someone more qualified and equipped to do the job. Like my buddy Jeremiah, I don't believe I am a great communicator, and yet, I write books, host a conversational podcast, and love to teach and share what I've learned to be true from God's Word with anyone who will listen.

But God is in the business of providing just what we need, when we need it, in order to fulfill the purpose he's designed us to fulfill.

In response to Jeremiah's excuses, God assured Jeremiah, "I am with you and will rescue you."[1]

In the days of Jeremiah, God's people, the Israelites, had forsaken God and his ways. God is the source of life, the "spring of living water,"[2] and rather than drink from the well of the God who had made them and was with them, they rebelled against him and decided to forge their own path and dig their own well. The result was absolute chaos and destruction. The nation of Israel was ultimately captured by the Assyrians and later the Babylonians. They became slaves of these nations and their freedom to worship God and live according to his ways and Word was taken from them.

Bible teacher Kelly Minter puts it this way: "Living outside of authority is actually not freedom at all."[3]

I know I'm out of alignment with God and his will when I desire the gifts and blessings of God more than the giver of those gifts and blessings. I know I'm digging my own well when I'm heavily burdened, confused, and anxious. When I feel trapped and unsure of my next move, I know I've got the shovel in my hand and am working to forge my own way.

On the contrary, recognizing the giver of all things keeps me in my lane, doing my thing.

Because of sin, we're inherently bent towards doing what we shouldn't do and often blindly believe that nothing bad will happen to us as a result.

When I lived in Boston, I witnessed the lake in the Boston Common park freeze over. Several signs were posted surrounding the lake that said not to walk or skate on the ice. And yet, every time I walked by the frozen lake, I saw people out walking or skating on it.

In Florida, I hear tales and see videos of people feeding alligators and even swimming near them.

No, thank you. But these are the types of crazy things we do if left to ourselves.

We are prone to wander right into danger and forsake the wonder of the one who made us.

In the story of the prodigal son, the son's pull toward his own way led him down a path of destruction and near death. Because of our sin nature, we all understand this pull. It's not hard to understand the wayward son, because our hearts are naturally wayward. What's harder for us to grasp and believe is that even in our wandering, even in the mess we can make for ourselves by choosing to surrender to our own way, Jesus is looking on, facing our direction, and beckoning us home, back to him and his way.

At first instance of us side-eyeing him, curious if he'll actually meet us when we're so far from the home path, he lifts his robe up off his ankles to free his feet, and he runs charging towards us to welcome us home. We are never too wayward, too far off the path, too lost, or too outside his reach. In his kindness, he will always find us, always welcome us home.

Jesus invites us to a life of flourishing, and it's found by finding our home with him and walking in obedience to his ways.

And here's the crazy part: Our obedience isn't anything we can produce on our own. Rather, it's the gracious outpouring from the Spirit of God of a life changed by the Word.

His kindness leads us to obedience.

My sons are most authentically themselves when they're home. They play and laugh and are free to be who God made them to be fully because they know they are home and home is where they can live without hinderance. And there are rules in our home. They know the limits. Yet, they are completely free because of the protection of those limits.

When they are obedient to the house rules, parameters, and structure of our home, they are free and our home is a place of authenticity, rest, and safety.

The same is true of our lives as we live in obedience to Jesus and his design.

Obedience is living into and out of the holy calling God has placed upon our lives. It is willingly giving up the temporary pleasures and gains of this world for the so-much-better eternal things.

What obedience is not is settling for instant gratification and immediate satisfaction. Rather, obedience is keeping our eyes fixed on Jesus and the hope and confidence of the not yet and what's to come.

Obedience is a call to freedom. It is the one-way path to freedom. There are no shortcuts. This is an invitation to be nearer to the Father than we imagined was possible. It's radical, stubborn grace, as my friend and author Kimberly Stuart calls it. *Stubborn* because it cannot be shaken in any way, shape, or form. It's swimming in the deep in full confidence and strength, absolutely sure God's got us.

I think too often we can confuse obedience with being told what to do.

When I was young, I never liked being told what to do. But now as an adult, I'd love it so much if someone told me exactly what to do. What to make for dinner (and if they stayed and cooked said dinner, even better). Which house to buy. What school to put the kids in. What church to attend. Which magnesium was the most effective. What to wear, like, every day.

Obedience has much more to do with living in freedom than it does with being told what to do.

When God created the Adam, Eve, and the garden of Eden, Adam and Eve were free to experience all the garden had to offer, except for the fruit of just one tree that God made clear they should avoid. They were free to flourish in Eden. It was only when they disobeyed that they lost their freedom.

The sly serpent caused Eve to believe that God's command to not eat of the Tree of the Knowledge of Good and Evil was his way of withholding goodness from her. But that's a lie.

The truth is that God's command to not partake of the tree's fruit was his way of protecting them. He is good and he protects his people.

The thing I think we have a hard time with, when it comes to obedience, is that we expect the outcome to be as we see fit. We are limited in our understanding, and yet, we tend to think that if and when we obey God and do what he says, the outcome will mean things go well with us and for us. We'll flourish.

But God never promises that our following him and his ways will lead to what we think is best.

I walked out of a Trader Joe's one afternoon

with a cart full of brown paper bags full of food. As I walked across the packed parking lot, a tiny, elderly man approached me with a limp in his step, a hunched-over back, and a small cardboard sign that indicated he was disabled and hungry.

I prayed a quick prayer in my mind: *Lord, do you want me to help this man?* Immediately, I felt a nudge to give him a banana that lay on top of one of the bags in the cart. I reached into the bag, removed a banana from the bunch, and handed it to the man. He was wearing a gray button-down shirt, and he put the banana in the chest pocket of his shirt and moved along.

After loading my beloved 4Runner with my grocery bags, I drove out of the parking lot and didn't think any more of the man or the banana. That is, until I sat at a red light adjacent to the Trader Joe's parking lot and spotted the man, apparently miraculously healed of his crippled walk, standing upright and walking perfectly well. He even had a bounce in his step and I watched in shock as he flung the banana in the air with his right hand as he walked.

I had been duped.

And I was angry. How could that guy pretend to be disabled and beg for money and food like that? I wanted my banana back.

And that's when I felt another nudge. Only this time, it wasn't about banana man, it was about me. Immediately, I felt as if the Lord was reminding me that the banana was not mine. In fact, it was his. I had not created the beautiful banana tree; he had. I had not caused the bananas to grow; he had. I had not provided the money to buy the banana at the store all on my own; he had enabled me to work and he had provided a job for me to work.

And in his kindness, I also heard the Lord say to me, "*It's not about the banana, Carrie. It's about you hearing my voice and trusting me with what you hear. It's about obedience to me. Listen for my voice. Trust me. Follow me.*"

The Lord grew me a bit that day, and I am forever grateful for his kindness to me. Had it not been for his voice and presence with me in that moment, I might have driven my 4Runner right over a curb or two and on over to banana man to give him a piece of my tiny mind. Instead, the Lord gave me an incredible gift: the gift of trusting his lead, following through with what he says, and not worrying about the outcome. That's his lane. I'm only to go where he leads. You and I don't control the outcomes.

Exhale. There is freedom in obedience.

Will I walk in obedience to Christ today or in accordance with how I feel? The answer is both on any given day. That's human. That's normal. And it's why the love, presence, and grace of Jesus is so very wild and scandalous: because it is not dependent upon what I do or don't do. The grace of Jesus covers all and is enough.

Friend, the freest place we could ever be is within the parameters Jesus designed. We don't have to fret about the what-ifs or how others may respond to our obedience. We get to take him at his word and trust that whatever he's speaking to us is for our best and the best of those around us. And almost always, the best isn't what we expect, but with Christ, it's better than we could ever imagine. Our obedience to Christ will always work out for good, because he is good and it will always draw us nearer and nearer to him, the end goal for any believer.

Jesus invites us to trust what he says and walk with him in obedience. In this way, he invites us to a life of freedom and flourishing.

CONCLUSION

A dear friend of mine, Mike, was on my podcast in May of 2025.[1] He shared his story of losing his job, his home, and his kid's school all in one day. Mike and his family lived in Altadena, CA, and watched in disbelief as their community burned to the ground in the Eaton Fire that decimated the area in January 2025.

It goes without saying, the loss was great and the grief ran deep.

Prior to that day of great loss, Mike was scheduled to preach to a room full of students at the end of the week. His sermon prep began before he lost his job, his house, and his kid's school.

The passage he had been preparing to preach on were these words from Paul found in Philippians:

> But whatever were gains to me I now consider

> loss for the sake of Christ. What is more, I consider everything a loss because of the surpassing worth of knowing Christ Jesus my Lord, for whose sake I have lost all things. I consider them garbage, that I may gain Christ.[2]

To Mike, who had just lost most of his belongings, his income, and his kid's school, these words from Paul were sobering, to say the least.

During our podcast conversation, Mike shared about how easy it is for us to like the idea of following Christ without facing the hardship of following. In fact, Mike asked the sobering question, "If you knew everything was going to be taken away in your pursuit of Christ, do you still want to sign up [to follow Christ]?"

If you didn't know the answer to that question when you picked up this book, I hope you have a confident *yes* answer by now.

Jesus lost it all on the cross so that we might gain all we are and need in him.

When he is true Lord of our lives, we can rest. We don't need to fret the small or big stuff.

When your gaze is upon Jesus, your perspective on and attitude about the things of this life shift dramatically.

It's why Paul could rejoice when he was imprisoned and why he kept working to advance the gospel of Jesus Christ even when he got the crap beat out of him continually.

When we find our rest hidden in Christ, losses of all kinds may come knocking at the door, but confidence and calm assurance, knowing and trusting Jesus will provide all we need, when we need it, will be our story.

When Jesus reminds us that the birds don't worry about their next meal, so how much more, then, do we not need to worry, these are not fluffy and empty words spoken simply to help us feel better about our circumstances. They are life and hope for our souls.

If you asked Mike today if would it be worth it to lose everything in exchange for knowing Christ, he would not hesitate one bit to say, yes, knowing Christ is worth any amount of loss.

That's ultimately what I hope you've been encouraged with as you've made your way through the pages of this book. I hope the flame of your walk with Christ has been fanned and you're feeling more seen, loved, and pursued by Jesus than you were before you read *Here for the Ride*.

I hope that as you read your Bible, the invitations Christ has extended throughout the whole of

Scripture jump off the pages and you see how inviting and hospitable he is toward you.

Jesus is creator, protector, provider, savior, rescuer, redeemer, restorer, friend, confidant, counselor, king, and so much more. We've merely scratched the surface of all of who he is and the constant and caring invitations he extends to us to know him more. Knowing him is the prize.

Mike would be the first to tell you that losing it all is a small price to pay for knowing Christ more and more.

Does that make loss any easier to swallow? Absolutely not. Life is hard and there is no softening its blows. But with Christ, even the worst of experiences work out for good. No matter what we go through in this life, it's his mercy and goodness that follow us all the days of our lives.

With Christ, we have his protection 24/7. We have his listening ear and his care regardless of what comes our way and whether it's good or bad.

Only Jesus has all authority over the circumstances in our lives, according to his will and way. We are simply along for the ride.

All we need and more is found in him and in him alone. That's not merely a flippant Christianese saying, it's a steady rock upon which we can cement our footing.

Jesus continually invites us to look to him for *all things* in all areas of life because he made you and I to be completely, 100% dependent upon him. He knows that sin causes us to feel as if we can handle life apart from him, and in his kindness, he is always present and graciously invites us toward him without end.

With all its whiplash, left turns, valley lows, and mountain highs, all of life is a journey back to him. All of life with him is a journey toward restoration.

On the daily, we make choices to either sync up with Jesus and to follow him or we go our own way. This is simply human nature. In full disclosure, most days, I don't even think about the choice I have to live for Jesus or myself. It's so natural to go about my day doing whatever I think is best, moment by moment. I rarely stop to consider what the one I call Lord of my life may think or want.

How might life be different if we didn't just go through the motions of the day, but instead of cruising on autopilot, we took the controls and created some margin to be mindful of how we're spending our time and what we're allowing to influence us, be it social media, news outlets, friends, or more?

How might life be different, more fulfilling, more purposeful, if we considered the reality that the King of Kings, Jesus, is present with us in all things? What if we paused long enough to check in with him on how he might want us to show up for the people in our lives throughout the day?

At the heart of every invitation Jesus extends to us is to the desire he has for you and me to know him more. We only touched upon ten invitations, but all of Scripture is an invitation to know God and to be known by him.

My hope for you as you've made your way through this book is that you've been encouraged to lean in to hear Jesus more clearly and to grow in your knowledge of and love for him.

He is with you. He is for you. He's crazy about you and he longs for you to know him.

Together, I hope we can say about our lives that we're just here for the ride and that we will follow where our kind and gracious Lord Jesus leads us. I believe this is the sweet spot of life, and I want it for you, for me, for my kids, and for all believers in the world.

May we live our lives palms up, with open

hands, free to receive and to give as the Lord sees fit.

After all, we're just *Here for the Ride*.

Acknowledgments

Writing is most definitely not a team sport. It's almost always done alone and yet it is never without the support and encouragement from a team of cheerleaders who believe in the one who pens the words. I write as a way to say thank you to those who have been in my corner without wavering and who continually believe my words are worth the ink they require to print.

And while I love using words to express gratitude and care, they never quite feel adequate for how I really feel. I can only trust and believe that Jesus will bless those in my corner beyond what my mere words can deliver.

In the meantime, I must thank the following friends who have been so gracious and kind to me.

Kalina, the Lord knew what he was doing when he chose you to befriend this crazy Californian upon her move to the great state of Texas. Your friendship during our Texas layover was an absolute gift in my life. Thank you for sharing your Topo Chico and love for *The Office* with me. I'm that much more blessed with you in my life.

Cindy, from the moment we met I knew we would be friends. Your love for plants and people is contagious. Acclimating to life in Florida was so much easier because of your kindness to me and my boys. You make everything better. I'm so grateful to call you friend.

Sylvia, you're wise and witty, gracious and generous, honest and humble. I look up to you and will forever thank God for allowing me to be your friend. Let's walk again soon.

Kaycee, I treasure you, sister. There may be six thousand miles of road between us, but I feel as close to you today as I did in the passenger side of your old school Honda Civic, blasting Shania Twain down the 405 Freeway. Thank you for being my friend.

Annette, you know you're in good company when you feel as if you've known someone forever, even when you really haven't. That's you, friend. Your love for the Good Shepherd is evident and I'm blessed to stand dependent upon him beside you.

Mom, you've been my biggest fan all my life. You're the best listener and encourager that ever lived. Thank you for loving me, the Pilot, and our boys so well. I'm proud and so grateful to call you mom.

Jesus, you continually invite me to know you more, even when I'm prone to wander off. I'm so grateful that you continually extend your mercy and grace my way. I only know freedom and flourishing because I know you. May my sons and their kids and all future generations of my family know your loving-kindness and say yes to the adventure of walking with you. You are so kind, and I love you.

Notes

Introduction: Here for the Ride

1. Carrie Ellen. *That's For Sure: Encouragement to Remain in the One Who Remains with Us*. Shining Roots Publishing, 2023.

2. John 14:6.

Chapter 1: The Invitation

1. Adele Ahlberg Calhoun. *Invitations from God: Accepting God's Offer to Rest, Weep, Forgive, Wait, Remember and More*. IVP, 2011.

2. 1 Peter 1:13.

Chapter 2: Invited to Slow Down

1. Psalm 116:2.

2. 1 Samuel 3:10. Read the entire story in 1 Samuel 3.

3. Corrie ten Boom, et al. *The Hiding Place*. Bantam, 1920.

Chapter 3: Invited to Lose Control

1. Colossians 1:15–17.
2. John 11:4.
3. John 11:21 and John 11:32.
4. John 11:25.

Chapter 4: Invited to Live the Better Way

1. Hebrews 4:12.
2. 2 Timothy 3:16.
3. Genesis 3:1.
4. This is just a snapshot of Psalm 119. Read the chapter in its entirety for more encouragement to stay kept in the only words that give life. (The verses quoted are verses 9–16.)

Chapter 5: Invited to Walk and Talk with Jesus

1. 3 John 1:4.
2. Hebrews 13:8.
3. 1 John 3:1.

Chapter 6: Invited to Cast Your Cares

1. 1 Peter 5:7.
2. Romans 5:8.
3. Hebrews 12:2.
4. 2 Corinthians 1:3–4.

Chapter 7: Invited to Today

1. Kelly Minter. *Finding God Faithful: A Study on the Life of Joseph.* Lifeway Press, 2019.
2. Genesis 41:1.
3. Dane Ortlund. *Surprised by Jesus: Subversive Grace in the Four Gospels.* Evangelical Press, 2021.

Chapter 8: Invited to Give it Up

1. See John 10:10.

Chapter 9: Invited to Peace

1. Judson W. Van DeVenter. "All to Jesus I Surrender." 1896. https://hymnary.org/hymn/PFTL1997/29.

Chapter 10: Invited to Run Home

1. Matthew 28:8.
2. John 20:16.
3. Emphasis mine.
4. Romans 10:15.
5. Romans 5:8.

Chapter 11: Invited to Flourish

1. Jeremiah 1:19.
2. Jeremiah 2:13.
3. Kelly Minter. *All Things New: A Study on 2 Corinthians*. Lifeway Press, 2016.

Conclusion

1. *That's For Sure with Carrie Ellen* podcast, episode 22. May 27, 2025.
2. Philippians 3:7–8.

More from Carrie

In *That's For Sure*, author Carrie Ellen connects personal, relatable stories with biblical truths to remind us that, despite life's uncertainties and unknowns, there are truths we can be absolutely sure of:

- You were made on purpose, for a purpose, and out of God's abundant love for you.
- You have everything you need today, because God is your provider.
- You can face tomorrow because you are never alone—God is always personally with you and steps ahead of you.

That's For Sure will encourage you, inspire you, make you laugh, and remind you that you can be confident God loves you, he is with you every single day, and he goes before you in all things.

That's For Sure is a conversational podcast hosted by author and speaker Carrie Ellen. Guests range from CEOs to authors, pastors to nonprofit leaders to actors and more. These ordinary and incredible men and women are up to story-worthy, life-changing acts in the world. Listen in wherever you listen to podcasts. You'll be encouraged and inspired. *That's For Sure.*

About the Author

Carrie is an author, podcast host, and dynamic speaker. She and her husband have been married for nearly twenty years, and she's a mom to two fun and funny boys and several beloved houseplants.

Carrie's been challenged and changed by God's Word, and as a result of coming to know the goodness of grace, she's determined to use her words to encourage people of all ages to draw near to Jesus.

Carrie holds an MA in World Missions and Evangelism from Gordon-Conwell Theological Seminary and a BA in Psychology from Vanguard University.

Connect with Carrie

 @carrie_ellen_live

 www.carrieellen.live

 carrieellen@carrieellen.live